German

A Complete Guide for German Language Learning Including German Phrases, German Grammar and German Short Stories for Beginners

Learn German

Step by Step Guide for Learning the Basics of The German Language

Table of Contents

Learn German

Introduction 7
Chapter 1: What it means to learn German 8
Chapter 2: Finding your passion for learning German 19
Chapter 3: Immersing yourself in German culture 25
Chapter 4: Finding native speakers to increase your overall understanding of the language and culture 38
Chapter 5: How to beat the most difficult part of learning the German language 44
Chapter 6: Learning German in a more formal classroom environment 52
Conclusion 55

German Phrases

Introduction 58
Chapter 1: Visiting Germany 60
Chapter 2: A Word About Pronunciation 62
Chapter 3: Nouns, Cases and Gender—Oh, my! 65
Chapter 4: Verbs 78
Chapter 5: Word Order 86
Chapter 6: Fundamental Vocabulary 90
Chapter 7: Basic Phrases 92
Chapter 8: Putting it All Together 124
Chapter 9: Continuing to Learn 126

German Short Stories

Introduction 131
Chapter One: Daisy Macbeth 133
Chapter Two: Die Andernacher Bäckersjungen (The Andernacher Baker Boy) 143
Chapter Three: Einkaufen im Supermarkt (Shopping in the Supermarket) 149
Chapter Four: Unser Haus (Our House) 153
Chapter Five: Die Suche nach Lorna (The Search for Lorna) 156
Chapter Six: Der Hausvater (The Householder) 162
Chapter Seven: Das Reiterbild in Düsseldorf (The Equestrian Picture in Dusseldorf) 169
Chapter Eight: Der Pfannkuchen (The Pancake) 175
Conclusion 190

© Copyright 2018 by Dave Smith - All rights reserved.

The following eBook is reproduced below with the goal of providing information that is as accurate and reliable as possible. Regardless, purchasing this eBook can be seen as consent to the fact that both the publisher and the author of this book are in no way experts on the topics discussed within and that any recommendations or suggestions that are made herein are for entertainment purposes only. Professionals should be consulted as needed prior to undertaking any of the action endorsed herein.
This declaration is deemed fair and valid by both the American Bar Association and the Committee of Publishers Association and is legally binding throughout the United States.

Furthermore, the transmission, duplication or reproduction of any of the following work including specific information will be considered an illegal act irrespective of if it is done electronically or in print. This extends to creating a secondary or tertiary copy of the work or a recorded copy and is only allowed with an expressed written consent from the Publisher. All additional rights reserved.

The information in the following pages is broadly considered to be truthful and accurate account of facts, and as such any inattention, use or misuse of the information in question by the reader will render any resulting actions solely under their purview. There are no scenarios in which the publisher or the original author of this work can be in any fashion deemed liable for any hardship or damages that may befall them after undertaking information described herein.

Additionally, the information in the following pages is intended only for informational purposes and should thus be thought of as universal. As befitting its nature, it is presented without assurance regarding its prolonged validity or interim quality. Trademarks that are mentioned are done without written consent and can in no way be considered an endorsement from the trademark holder.

Introduction

Thank you and congratulations on downloading *Learn German*. The German language is the 11th most widely spoken language on earth with 92 to 95 million native speakers around the globe composing 1.39% of the world's population. By downloading this book, you are taking the first steps in your own personal conquest in learning this great and storied language. The following chapters will be more of a general outline on what steps to take when first learning the language and how to develop and apply the skills necessary to master German.

Here are some of the topics which will be discussed within this brief book:

- What it means to learn Standard German, High German, and Low German;
- Finding your passion for learning German;
- Turning a chore into inspiration;
- Learning German by immersing yourself deeply in the German culture;
- Finding native speakers to improve your overall understanding of the language and its culture;
- How to overcome the most difficult part of learning the German language; and finally
- Learning German in a more formal class environment.

These following chapters will, more precisely, discuss the study techniques applicable to learning a new language, the culture of Germany as well as the rest of German speaking Europe, some of the history of the language and its various dialects, steps for beginning the study of the language, and learning German inside and outside of formal class settings.

There are a number of books on the market very similar to this one. Thank you again for choosing this one and if you enjoy it or find it helpful, a review on Amazon would be very much appreciated.

Chapter 1: What it means to learn German

Standard German, Low German, and High German

Learning German

Learning a foreign language is, to the inexperienced, one of intimidating tasks that education has to offer and, to the polyglot, one of the rewarding and advantageous tasks that education can make a person do. As with developing any new skill set, learning a language takes lots of time, effort, and practice, but once the brain starts to make the new connections necessary for progress and the learner starts to build confidence and skill, the transition from intermediate to fluent can be a lot smoother than the transition from beginner to intermediate. The learning curve can increase exponentially.

The contemporary world is more globalized and interconnected than it ever has been. This is a fact that extols the practicality of learning a second language. But the reasons for learning go beyond just geopolitics, they vary widely. We should now examine some of the innumerable benefits of learning a second language:

1. Connection
Multilingualism breaks down barriers that are very real to monolingual people. In learning a second language, there is constant opportunity to expand horizons and make connections with new people which would have been out of question beforehand.

2. Career Advancement
Multilingualism doubles as a major competitive advantage in virtually any line of work. Not only will it help you on getting hired, but it also statistically increases salary and benefits. As far as employment is concerned, there is no down side to learning a second language.

3. Cognitive Benefits

This is a big one. This might be the biggest benefit of learning a new language as it affects the learner the most profoundly. While the cognitive benefits of learning a language are too multifarious to all be mentioned within this book, some very important ones include: problem-solving and critical thinking skills, improved memory, ability to multitask, enhanced concentration, as well as better listening skills. Multilinguals also switch between monitor changes and competing tasks within their environments more easily than those who only speak one language. They also age more gracefully, with cognitive decline being staved off among the multilingual.

4. Exploring Other Cultures

To connect to a language is, in part, an effort to connect with the culture which surrounds the language. Learning another language can help teach the synthetic history and culture of a people, exposing the inquisitive student to every phase of activity such as tradition, religion, politics, philosophy, art, morals, and many more just through one medium.

5. Seeing the World through a Broader Lens

Multilingualism can make travelling around the world seem like an entirely different ballgame. Monolingual tourists tend to get trapped in tourist bubbles, only being allowed access to the aspects of the culture that foreigners get, while never getting the bigger picture that only the native language speakers can provide. Learning the language can open doors especially in terms of getting to know other people. Learning it can also provide more opportunities for studying and working abroad.

6. Seeing the Source

In the internet age, it is easy to confound fantasy with reality. When it comes to foreign nations, the internet (or any other source) can simply not compare to the real thing in terms of value, importance, or accuracy. Learning a language is a great key to the heart of the nation, and accuracy of one's understanding of it.

7. Becoming a Polyglot
Learning a second language is a useful feat, multiplying vocabulary and improving communication skills in one's native language. Learning languages beyond the second, however, has surprisingly been shown to be easier than it is the first time around. This is especially true for children; they are nature's greatest linguists. Once the neural networks involved in the process of new language acquisition have been primed, it is much easier for people to pick up more and more words from more and more obscure vernaculars.

8. A Major Boost of Confidence
At least as far as Americans are concerned, multilingualism is tantamount regality, and those who can display the skill have been shown to receive massive gains of social currency. While the inevitable mistakes which are made in the process of learning the language can tend to damage one's ego, these are offset by the self-worth gains that come with the territory. To learn a new language is an act of escaping one's comfort zone. After all, it is the satisfaction of learning a new language that can and will get the learner through the difficult precipitate phase of learning.

9. The Strengthening of Decision Making Abilities
Interestingly enough, it has been proven that decisions made in a person's second language are much more reason-based than those made in the native language. It is always funny how life always leaves us with more reason as time goes by. When deliberations are made in second and third tongues, emotional responses and biases connected with our mother tongue leave our thinking patterns more readily. It becomes much easier to be objective when speaking new languages because baggage dissolves and all that is left are facts and stratagem.

10. The Gaining of Perspective
As people embark on new journeys into novel cultures and places, familiarity always catches the senses. Common threads are observed

by people that came out of their comfort zones and stayed there for a while. When this happens, it gives the much needed perspective on our native culture by making the learner reexamine things familiar to them in new lights. This is similar to measures taken by many dream therapists when dealing with patients with childhood baggage. The aspects of their dreams are asked to be described as if the patient were describing them to someone from another planet. By doing this, the patient can gain perspective on what inhabits their dreams and how they really feel about the things that they are exposed to in their waking lives. It gives opportunity to see the things around them in a new light and travelling abroad can do just that as well.

All the reasons for learning a foreign language listed above apply to any given language, but the next portion of this chapter will discuss the inner workings of the German language.

German

The Germanic language family is a very wide one which encompasses a wide variety of languages and dialects. The three major branches within this family are West Germanic languages, North Germanic languages, and East Germanic languages. Together, these branches are spoken by approximately 515 million people worldwide. Most of these people, however, reside in Europe.

The first branch to be mentioned here is the western branch of languages. This branch includes German, Dutch, English, Afrikaans (a descendant of Dutch), Low German, Yiddish, Scots, Limburgish varieties (with speakers along the borders of the Netherlands, Belgium, and Germany), and Frisian languages (with speakers in the Netherlands and Germany).

The northern branch is a much smaller one. Its languages include Icelandic, Norwegian, Swedish, Faroese, and Danish.

Lastly, we come to the Eastern branch of the language and are met by a graveyard of European tongues. The languages of this branch include Gothic, Vandalic, and Burgundian. All of these languages are now extinct, and the last one of them to die was the Crimean Gothic, which went in the late 18th century in rural parts of Crimea.

By most estimates, this family of languages consists of 48 individual living languages. Of these 48, 41 are listed as West Germanic languages, 6 are North Germanic languages, and 1 other language residing in Brazil which is the Riograndenser Hunsrükisch German, usually falls into neither category. It is now impossible to say just how many languages have been a part of this family throughout the course of history. Many of them, especially the East German languages, died out during or after the migration period following the decline of the Roman Empire between the fourth and sixth centuries A.D. Some West Germanic languages died out during this period as well, Lombardic would be one example.

World War 2 changed lots of things, including the German language. In linguistics, a *sprachraum* is defined as being a geographical region in which a common first language along with its dialect varieties is spoken. The *sprachraum* of the German family of languages suffered heavy losses in both area and speaker population as a result of World War 2. Meanwhile, the 21st century hasn't been much better for these dialects because many of them are dying out to make room for Standard German and its massive popularity in these regions.

The patriarch of this massive family is what was known as Proto-Germanic, or Common Germanic. This was a language spoken around the middle of the first millennium B.C. in what history remembers as Iron Age Scandinavia. This language, along with its numerous ancestors, is known for having a great number of linguistic features peculiar to it. One famous example among these is what is known as Grimm's Law. It is a consonant change completely unique to the Germanic family of languages. This Proto-Germanic language was later followed up by many varieties of the tongue, which travelled south of Scandinavia when several Germanic tribes in the 2nd century B.C. conquered and settled in many parts of modern northern Germany and southern Denmark.

A fourth century A.D. translation of the New Testament into Gothic is the earliest Germanic text known to history. This text was translated by Ulfilas, a Cappadocian Greek who worked as a missionary and bishop. Around the 10th century, the dialects varied so much that inter comprehensibility had become impossible, which is still true to this day. Again, the migration period culled off the East German languages, but they continued to influence the languages that surrounded them by assimilating themselves near their respective ends.

The middle ages then saw West German languages split between those which observed the new consonant shift, and those which didn't. The North German languages, on the other hand, stayed essentially united.

Any changes which occurred during and after (if such a time exists) the age of reason are relatively miniscule and more or less subordinate to those made beforehand. Most of these newer changes are due to standardization decrees and solutions to ongoing problems regarding certain aspects of the existing languages; Germanic languages are not born or culled off anymore, at least not for now.

Standard German

The first subset of the German language that it is necessary to go over here is so-called 'standard' German. This is a variety of the German language that has undergone standardization and is a common means of communication between some certain dialect areas. It is what was known as a Dachsprache or an Ausbau language serving as an independent variety of the language with other Abstand or dependent language varieties related to it. The role that Ausbau languages play for linguistics is that of builder-out or patriarch of other languages in the family.

Standard German did not start out as a dialect common across multiple regions. It took hundreds of years to evolve as a written language, with its writers constantly making changes to it for its widespread comprehension. At around 1800, the people of northern Germany that are speakers of Low Saxon languages, started to learn the language as a foreign one. It later traveled southward and completely annihilated many of the languages of southern Germany, leaving only some small and scattered enclaves of Low German in its wake. Ever since, it has remained the standard language of Germany and her people, uniting a wide variety of tribes and dialects under one cultural blanket. As of today, though, these local dialects are usually only used in informal and private speech, commonly limited to home settings.

There are a few nations that this language inhabits, and the language differs slightly in every single one. These countries are: Austria, Switzerland, and Germany. In addition to these variances, there are different varieties of Standard German within the nation of Germany. These varieties of Standard German differ mostly from one another in vocabulary and pronunciation, although in some cases variance occurs in grammar and orthography. The different varieties of the language are not so clearly discerned in written language, but their variances shine through more vividly when spoken.

The variations of Standard German are, however, not to be confused with the various dialects of German, despite their similarities and influence to each other. The main thing that separates the two is the fact that the varieties of the Standard German language stem from the common tradition of the written German language. The local dialects, on the other hand, have roots that go back much further than Standard German, before the unification of the written German language and, in the case of low German, these dialects can belong to entirely different languages.

The Standard German language has undergone numerous standardization changes within its lifespan. This started way back in the 16th century, with the Luther Bible of 1534. These changes continued up until 2006, when the last one occurred over disputes about spelling and the splitting of German words. These will probably continue in the future, as language is an entity that undergoes constant evolution.

Low German

Low German is what is known as a West German Language and it is most commonly spoken in two regions: Northern Germany and the northeastern region of The Netherlands. Being most closely related to Frisian and English, this language is part of the Ingaevonic or North Sea Germanic group of West Germanic languages.

The dialects of Low German spoken in The Netherlands are referred to only as being Low Saxon, but, on the other hand, the dialects of northwestern Germany (Bremerhaven, Bremen, Hamburg, Westphalia, Schleswig-Holstein, and Lower Saxony) can be referred to as either being Low Saxon or Low German. Those spoken in northeastern Germany are exclusively Low German. These differences are a result of history; northwestern Germany as well as The Netherlands were once settlements of The Saxons, while northeastern Germany was not.

Old Saxon is the grandfather of Low German. It was spoken between the 9th and 12th centuries by the Saxon inhabitants of northwest Germany and Denmark. This language was survived by Middle Low German, spoken between 1100 and 1600. This language was neighbored by Middle Dutch in the west and by Middle High German in the south. Middle Low German is important historically because it served the Hanseatic league—a confederation of guilds and market towns throughout northwestern Europe in the late 1100s—as its *Lingua Franca* or *bridge language,* which supplied a common tongue throughout the confederation.

And to that end, we reach the contemporary situation of Low German. The Dutch and German dialects remain detached, and the decision to exclude the teaching of Low German throughout the schools of Germany was met with bitter opposition by some. Proponents of the teaching of the language argued on the point of its dense historical and cultural significance that it should remain in formal education. Meanwhile, High German had already become the widely used language in education, science, politics, and national unity. It was no wonder that High German would eventually win the day.

Low German has always played second fiddle to High German. Known for its archaic constructions and features, many linguists find this language backward and of limited use. Public reverence coupled with tradition have, however, kept the language afloat though. Today, while not being widely used in academia or in the professional world, Low German still finds itself in the homes of thousands of German speakers in spite of its supposed shortcomings. And, while it is still not widely taught, it also finds itself within the schools of Germany and The Netherlands.

High German

And finally, we at last come to Low German's more popular cousin, High German. High German refers to a variety of German dialects spoken in central as well as southern Germany, Austria, Switzerland, Liechtenstein, and Luxembourg. It also encompasses dialects spoken within regions of France (northern Lorraine and Alsace), The Czech Republic (Bohemia), Italy (south Tyrol), and Poland (upper Silesia). As with other European dialects, these ones are also spoken within various diaspora across the globe, namely in Romania, The United States, Brazil, Russia, Argentina, Chile, Mexico, and Namibia.

The main thing that differentiates High German from other forms of German dialects is the famous High German consonant shift.

The term 'High' German derives from the highlands of Germany, where these dialects originate from. This class of languages includes the famous Yiddish language of the Ashkenazi community of Jews in central Europe, standard German, and Luxembourgish. These aforementioned highlands of Germany are not limited to German soil however. They also include Luxembourg, Liechtenstein, Austria, and most of Switzerland. Meanwhile, its cousin Low German refers to dialects spoken in the lowlands of Germany and the Netherlands, along the coasts of the North German Plain.

This dialect can trace its roots back to around 500 A.D. in Old High German. In Old High German, two varieties, Swabian and East Franconian, became the dominant court and poetry languages of the House of Hohenstaufen around 1200. This term 'High German' introduces itself to history around 1400 in Upper Saxony, Swabia, Bavaria, Franconia, and Austria. This language triumphed over all those around it and continues to triumph today as an important basis of the German language.

It would now be wise to look over the family tree that all these dialects of German stem from. The other variants of the German language which have been mentioned previously are all related to this one, and is found within the large barge of central European languages. This tree of languages is roughly as follows:

Central German:
East Central German-
Upper Saxon
Thuringian
Lausitzisch-Neumärkisch
High Prussian
Silesian
West Central German-
Central Franconian
Moselle Franconian
Ripuarian
Rhine Franconian
Palatine
Hessian
High Franconian:

East Franconian
South Franconian
Upper German:
    Alemannic-
Low Alemannic
High Alemannic
Highest Alemannic
Swabian
    Bavarian-
Central Bavarian
Northern Bavarian
Southern Bavarian
Hutterite German
Cimbrian
Yiddish
Lombardic (extinct)

Chapter 2: Finding your passion for learning German

Studying outside of what is required in school can seem somewhat intimidating and time consuming. A great number of people seem to get the idea that informal and or unguided study can muddy up intellectual waters or otherwise just make it harder to learn. There are some grains of truth in this presumption, although in other cases, informal study can be more beneficial and efficient than its formal counterpart. It all depends on the student's erudition, work ethic, and grit more than anything. While it is typically advisable to study German (or any other subject for that matter) with some sort of teacher or tutor guiding you through the process, it remains more important that the student genuinely enjoys and takes an active interest in the field of study.

In this chapter we will take some time to discuss some studying tips and techniques that certainly prove to be useful when studying German, or any other subject for that matter.

The first, and a very important tip about studying that should be mentioned here is the practice of breaking the material, whatever it may be, into chunks that are more easily digestible. This is a practice that is especially useful for working on a task that seems overwhelming. Once the material has been carved out into smaller sections, those individual sections can be studied with more ease from day to day. This can take superfluous pressure off of the student and allow for better focus on the tasks at hand.

Another important tip would be to reward yourself for hard work done. It doesn't, after all, make someone self-indulgent or weak to reap the rewards of his or her labor. These small rewards can actually be beneficial and can be done in the forms of short walks, small blocks of phone time, or maybe even the occasional snack in between longer periods of study.

Human beings are creatures of habit, which is exactly why it can be extremely useful to create a routine of creating your own study time (or work hours for that matter). These habits, in fact, can become so strong that it can even become difficult for a student to be able to relax for the day without studying first. With constant and prolonged self-discipline, any given person can become a student to be reckoned with, leaving all competition in the dust. Studies show, however, that it takes 20 to 30 days on average to form a habit, which is why self-discipline should be duly emphasized.

For those still in school, it is important to be clear with yourself when it comes to why you want to get good grades. It is always easier to meet your goals when there is a general idea of why those goals should be met. One useful method of doing this is making a list of academic and personal goals, for example:

I would like to develop myself and learn more.
I would like to get into more useful habits.
I would like to become more disciplined and focused as a student.
I would like to get into a good school.
I would like to have a good career one day.
I would like to provide for my family and those who are close to me in the future.
I would like to have certainty that I'm doing all that I can in my endeavors.
I would like to live as regret free as I possibly can.

Writing goals and aspirations down can give perspective and direction for the student. Also, the lists made can serve as reminders and motivators in the future.

The use of mind maps is a very good skill for students to have. Unlike lists, mind maps allow interconnectivity that the brain always craves. These can be used for any subject and under any circumstances and the outcomes always remain fruitful. The brain makes connections naturally, and mind maps not only assist in this process, but also defines and clarifies the connections made.

Another tip would be to try to always make a boring subject seem and feel as interesting as possible. This one can be particularly useful in learning German as many often consider learning foreign languages boring. It is always important, however, to stave off boredom when studying like the disease that it is. There are many methods of doing this successfully, but the most important one would be to re-engage yourself. No subjects are ultimately very boring at all as long as people just look over them with disinterested minds. It is always important to simply dig a little deeper every time the student feels like yawning.

It is always more advantageous, and also more rewarding, to come to understand topics rather than just memorizing their contents. Rote memorization can take a learner quite far, and there are always some bastions of employing this in your study habits, but in more advanced studies and inquisitive minds, it becomes increasingly important to grasp the material at hand as reference to other subjects. This is also more important than memorization because it actually makes room for critical thinking and the application of facts. In learning German, there is always emphasis placed on vocabulary, but there is also emphasis placed on actually putting the words together to make statements that makes sense.

Another important practice in learning is to always be on the lookout for personal knowledge gaps as well as thinking errors. There is, after all, no room for competence, or in this case fluency, where there remains an overabundance of mistakes. Staying cognizant of errors in learning will not only curtail mistakes and misunderstandings, but it will also deepen the student's understanding of the subject matter at hand.

Studying in shorter increments of time is always beneficial as well. This study habit has been shown to be more effective than others. It is what is known as *spaced* learning, and its advantages are attributed to the way memories are formed. Neurons have to be left alone for periods of time in between study for memories to be properly embedded within the links between them. This is why it is always beneficial to avoid cramming, so spaced learning would naturally be the best method of studying for the mind.

The Pomodoro Technique is a very famous yet not very widely used technique in learning. Its most basic and most common structure are as follows:

1. Decide on the task that you need to work.
2. Time yourself within a 25-minute increment .
3. Start working on the task.
4. Stop working once the 25-minute mark has been reached.
5. Checkmark a piece of paper.
6. If you are up to fewer than four check marks, then you must take a 3 to 5-minutes break, repeat from step one when your break has been completed.
7. After four check marks, or Pomodoros, have been met, you must then take a 15 to 30-minute break.
8. Draw a line crossing off the four check marks and start over again

This technique keeps the study blocks short and on point so that knowledge is retained well and the student is not fatigued.

Another important piece of advice is the fact that motivation should be expected to come frequently or readily. As strange as it may seem, motivation can generally come more readily when it is not expected or desired so much. It appears well by contrast, as with any other mood. No one among us feels motivated all the time, so it is not advisable to rely on feelings of motivation to retain the ability on getting things done. This is why it is more important to keep a strict routine and work through the boredom that surrounds studying.

It is important, maybe beyond any other tips listed here, to exercise the brain. In doing this, it can be helpful to look at the brain as a muscle than an organ because it gives more of an impression of adaptability. Developing one's ability to focus is like any other form of personal development where in it takes constant practice and unflappable determination. It's like becoming a great athlete, it takes

thousands of hours of practice that is set on a rigid schedule over the course of years. The only real difference is that it is the mind being worked out rather than the body. Some great means of developing this skill are challenging world issues, writing journals, or solving puzzles. The greater and wider the variety of ways that your brain is challenged, the stronger and more powerful it will become.
Here are some websites with great resources for training the brain: Luminosity, NeuroNation, and Brain HQ.

The roles of rest and recovery are also not to be underestimated in study. It is always important to get at least 8 hours of sleep each and every night, no matter what you spend your waking hours doing. There are also certain foods which are better for the health of the brain than others. Some foods that offer fatty acids which the brain needs to function properly are as follows:

Nuts, avocados, salmon, berries, beans, pumpkin seeds, pomegranate juice, and dark chocolate.

This next piece of advice ties in with the concept on creating a study routine very well. This one would be to organize your time. With creating a study schedule comes lots of commitment, and where commitment goes, motivation usually follows. It is always much easier to stay with a topic to keep an organized schedule. Here are some steps in creating a reliable study schedule:

1. Make a list of tasks which you need to complete for every subject that you study.
2. Try downloading a study schedule template or making one by hand. You can then block of available times for independent study.
3. Try to keep things simple and easy to remember by choosing blocks of time that remain the same throughout each day of the week.
4. Create a plan for every day which includes the most important tasks that the day has to offer, then make sure to stick to it religiously.

At the end of each week, or any allotted time frame, you can then track the progress that you have made. You may then be pleasantly surprised by your results, and if you are not, then you can always keep trying to make adjustments to whatever you need to to meet your goals.

The results of all these methods mentioned will ultimately all be dependent upon how hard the student tries. With that being said, it is always important to remain active in your learning experiences rather than passive. Passive learning takes on the presumption that the learner is a blank slate, but many attests that the best way to learn is to immerse oneself in learning completely. Here are some steps in doing this more effectively:

Finding applications of topics within your normal life
Performing case studies to test ideas and concepts
Group projects
Brainstorming on ways to apply the concepts learned to the issues that you come across

All of these tips can be applied not only in your pursuit of learning German, but to virtually any subject the student takes up. German is one of the most important and useful languages of modernity, and in addition, it is a relatively easy language to learn for the native English speaker. By using these techniques in learning German or any other subject, the student will not only learn the subject with more ease, but also use the tools gained here to help him or her to develop other skills in the future. These are concepts that are stuck out of time and place. It is always much more useful to know how to learn than what to learn. Education is a constantly evolving chapter within a student's life, and one that can never quite be mastered, but can be rode to greater heights with proper practice and skill.

Chapter 3: Immersing yourself in German culture

German Culture
Germany is very much the center of Europe in more ways than just geographically. It also serves as the center of European economic and political activity. Germany is Europe's second
most populous country in terms of overall population, behind Russia. In fact, the World Factbook estimates its population to be around 80 million people. Germany's economy also boasts impressive figures as well. It is, in fact, the largest one within the continent and the fifth largest one on the face of the globe.

Germany not only is home to an extremely large population, but it also exerts influence over many smaller nations that border it. These include Belgium, Czech Republic, Austria, Denmark, Luxembourg, France, Switzerland, The Netherlands, and Poland. All of these cultures listed have had reciprocal influence on and from Germany.

Unsurprisingly, the population of Germany is around 91.5%. It may, however, come as a bit of a shock to learn that the second largest ethnic group is actually Turkish at about 2.4% of the nation's population. This leaves a remaining 6.1% accounted to the different groups of ethnic Greek, Italian, Russian, Serbo-Croatian, and Spanish people. It is the city life which most of Germany's people are drawn to. However, roughly 75.7% of the population residing in urban areas.

The Germans are a very staid and conservative people, placing high values on the virtues of structure, punctuality, and privacy. Some of the stereotypes surrounding Germany and her people hold true in these few respects. They also place very high quotas on hard work, industriousness, and thriftiness. It takes a lot to make Germans comfortable, usually. They often need to have the ability to organize and compartmentalize the world into well-kept units, as they are a very pragmatic people. They therefore tend to manage their time rather carefully, with calendars, schedules, and agendas taking precedence over any spontaneity that life's vicissitudes have to offer.

The Germans often get the reputation of being rather stoic people. This is understandable as they do tend to strive for precision and perfection in nearly every aspect of their day to day lives. This is not always such a bad trait to have though. In fact, it's often a great one that has lots of practical benefits. Civilizations often begin as stoic and end up being epicurean. It could be argued that the only thing more destructive than access stoicism is mindless pleasure seeking. They seldom hand out compliments to others and even less seldom admit faults, even jokingly. These are aspects of their stoicism that could be criticized. All of these factors may coalesce to make these people seem unfriendly, but the Germans actually have very highly developed social consciences and keen senses of community.

Language
The main language of Germany, which is unsurprisingly German, has many different offshoots previously mentioned. Standard German is spoken by a landslide 95% of the population. Several minor languages including Low German, High German, Dutch, Frisian variances, and many more are also spoken in Germany.

Religion
Like the vast majority of the western world, Christianity dominates the land for centuries. This religion is followed by 65 to 70% of the nation. With that figure, Catholics comprise 29% of them. Meanwhile, Muslims are a small minority, as in lots of other European nations, accounting for 4.4% of the total population. The remaining 36% of the population are not religious or does not observe a religion other than those two previously mentioned.

The two largest churches in Germany are the Roman Catholic Church, and the Evangelical Church. Their Evangelical Church is a confederation of Protestant (Lutheran and Reformed) churches. Those two churches comprise the 65 to 70% of the nation. In 2016,

Orthodox Christianity made up for around 2% of the overall population.

The religious makeup of the nation of Germany differs greatly with a number of factors, namely region and age. As could probably be expected, the youth are now less religious than their elders. In fact, the majority of Germany's population under 25 now claim to hold no religious belief. Another trend that is common in Germany, and also in many parts of the world, is the inverse correlation between urban living and religiosity. In fact, in many major German cities, Berlin and Hamburg for example, non-religious people comprise the majority of citizenry. As far as states are concerned, however, it is the Eastern states which hold the least religious belief. A majority of 60-70% classify as holding no religious belief in these states. Some of these figures seem surprising in contrast to American religiosity, but the culture of Germany doesn't seem to suffer much from the variance.

As is the case for most of the globe, Germany started out with polytheistic paganism and eventually adopted Christianity later. This occurred only in prehistoric Germany and parts of Scandinavia. The concept of a united German land just did not exist until Julius Caesar, invading Gaul, sought to destroy the increasingly united Germanic tribes above him. This primitive religion included Gods such as Thor, Odin, Freyja, and Baldr.

After the 4th century, in the regions of southern Germany which had then been occupied as part of the Roman Empire, early Christianity began to take hold and replaced the old Gods. Never again would these Gods rule German soil. Pagan temples and ways of life were then replaced by Christian churches and morality to uphold the sudden transition.

It was until the Carolingian Period, however, that Christianity began to take its hold over the German mainland. The main person responsible for this invasion was Charlemagne, with his swift military invasions followed by his conversion tactics. One great example of religious structures built during this time period is the Palace of Aachen, built during Charlemagne's reign.

The Germany of the middle ages then saw very little to virtually no change in its religious institutions. The majority of the region remained Roman Catholic and, for the most part, busied itself with issues other than official religion.

In 1517, Martin Luther published his 95 Theses, one of the most Seminole documents ever written throughout the history of the world. Its main objective was the criticism of the Roman Catholic Church for its selling of indulgences (payments made to clergy to atone for sins) along with other abuses of power.

Not only was Luther opposing how the clergy abused their powers at that time, but he was also opposing the very idea of the papacy. The Reformation is significant in that it is the first open criticism or reaction to the corruption and misguidance of the Roman Catholic Church known to history. The publication of the theses was quickly followed up by the Diet of Worms in 1521, which outlawed Luther. The Reformation continued regardless and would not rest until it had consumed all of Europe open to its teachings. Luther followed up by then translating the bible from Latin to German, making it readable and accessible to all people of all German speaking regions of Europe, not just the clergy. This in turn made the bible much more approachable to Europe and gave the Roman Catholic Church much less power of its teachings. Today, the denominations of Christianity are so numerous that no one has very much theological power over the religion. How Luther turns out to be important in linguistic history is the fact that the dialect that he translated the bible into was not by any means a widespread or popular one before his translation, now it has evolved into Standard German.

After the Thirty Years War, there was a widespread effort to unite the larger Lutheran and the smaller Reformed Protestant Churches. This occurred in Prussia, with King Frederick William III's motivation being the unification of all protestant churches within the nation under the crown. This was done with several complications, and eventually Frederick William IV had to give the 'Old' Lutherans the right to separate from this conglomeration in an effort to keep peace among the public.

This point in religious history marks a widespread attitude shift in relation to God. The Roman Catholic Church placed more emphasis on worship, ceremony, and the church, but followers of the new denominations were searching for more personal relationships with God. The German people, whether out of hubris or out of need for personal growth, started to see God as wanting a personal relationship with his children. This is a view that many of these denominations still hold today.

As the rationalism of the 18th century eventually faded away, the individualism of the 19th century continued to shape Germany's concept of God. All of this was, of course, met by fierce opposition from Catholics still loyal to the papacy. There was then a controversy surrounding children of mixed marriages. There was no consensus on what the legal religion of children born to both Catholic and Protestant parents should be. After some deliberation, it was decided that these children should always be raised Protestant. This differed from the Napoleonic laws previously set in place which ordered that the parents should be the one making the decision on what will be the religion of mixed children.

The most crucial blow to the power of the papacy, however, came in the human form of Otto von Bismarck, who flatly refused to tolerate any given power base outside of Germany to have a say in German affairs. Bismarck launched a so called 'culture war' against the power of the pope in 1873, which gained lots of support among German liberals opposing the power of the church.

From that point on, although they comprised about a third of the German population, Catholics were not allowed to hold most offices within the German and Prussian governments. This is, however, overshadowed by the fact that after 1871 a systematic purge of

Catholics began within the two nations. In fact, the interior ministry at the time only staffed one Catholic boy in total. Another religious minority discriminated against the Jews throughout this time.

One of the ways in which this purge of Catholics was achieved was through what is now known as the Pulpit Law. This law prohibited the use of speech by clergy which in any way displeased the government. Many officials within the Roman Catholic Church were openly against this law, and many of them were imprisoned or exiled as a result.

Bismarck did, however, severely underestimated the power and tenacity of the Catholic people in their resistance to his exclusive laws. The Catholic Church promptly denounced these new laws and called upon its followers in all parts of Germany to protest the treatment. An uneasy peace was eventually established as some of these laws were repealed, but several discriminatory laws regarding education and work were left in place.

The newly formed Weimar Republic established a constitution for itself in 1919 which not only did not include any official state religion, but also guaranteed freedom of faith and religion to all its citizens. Earlier in German history, these freedoms had only been mentioned in the constitutions of some individual states. Catholics and Protestants were finally equal under the letter of the law with this new constitution. The German Freethinkers League was then established. It was comprised of 500,000 members, mostly atheist. Nazi leadership did, fittingly enough, shut this group down later in 1933.

The year 1933 marked one of the most important and devastating times in the history of Germany. In January of that year, Adolf Hitler's Nazi Party seized control of the German government seeking to assert state control over the churches among other things. Two social responses to this were the Positive Christianity and Deutsche Christen movements, which both sought to the tenants of National Socialism with the Christian religion. These movements had mixed successes until the late 1936, when gradual worsening of relations between the church and state caused many to abandon the churches. There were no official policies regarding church membership within the Nazi government, but many officials started to leave their churches in droves around this time. Jews at this time were, as the reader already knows, increasingly marginalized as well.

The conclusion of World War 2 saw the German state divided into two parts: East and West. West Germany was now controlled by the western allies, namely England, America, France, and Canada. Eastern Germany, on the other hand, was now controlled by the U.S.S.R. East and West Germany now took two completely different approaches on the issue of religious freedom. West Germany, otherwise known as the Federal Republic of Germany, adopted a constitution in 1949 which stated that no citizen was to be discriminated against on the basis of their faith or religious beliefs, and that no official state religion was to be established. East Germany, also known as the German Democratic Republic, adopted a communist system which aimed to drastically reduce the role of religion in the society. Christian churches, regardless of denomination, were restricted by the government. This explains the aforementioned tendency of eastern German states to be less religious. The implications of soviet policies are still seen today.

German religious communities of a sufficient size and stability that happen to be loyal to the constitution are what is known as statutory corporations. These communities are given special privileges under the constitution. Included within these is the right for state schools to give religious instruction within these communities. They are also subject to having membership fees collected (for various fees) by the national revenue department known as 'church taxes'. These taxes are surcharges between 8 and 9% of the income tax. This differs from many other western nations which don't typically tax their churches. This high status applies mainly to the Roman Catholic Church, the mainline Protestant Evangelical Church in Germany, various free churches throughout the nation, and a small number of Jewish communities. There is also the ongoing discussion over whether or not to allow Muslims and other minority religious groups into this system as well.

In 2018, representatives from Schleswig-Holstein, Hamburg, Lower Saxony, and Bremen have come together to conclude that a decision on whether or not to make Reformation Day an official holiday permanently was desperately needed to be ratified by their state parliaments. This initiative began after the 500th anniversary of the reformation in 2017. It also stems, in part, from the fact that the northern German states now have far less holidays annually than many of the southern states do. Also during this year, the states of Schleswig-Holstein, Hamburg, Lower Saxony, and Bremen all adopted resolutions and made it an official holiday.

In contemporary times, Protestantism dominates the north and east of Germany and Catholicism dominates the south and west. The decline of Christianity in the late 20th and early 21st centuries, coupled with the state atheism of the former German Democratic Republic, have merged to create an extremely secular culture in northeastern Germany. The late 20th and the early 21st centuries have, however, brought immigrants from a wide variety of foreign lands and they brought with them lots of religions and beliefs that are new to the nation. These include Eastern Orthodox Christianity and Islam.

Cuisine
German cuisine may often be overshadowed by its neighbors such as France, Italy, and even England, but that does not imply that German cuisine is by any means worse. German cuisine is probably most widely known for its hardiness and its boldness. It's also more meat-oriented as compared to many of its European cousins. Of all meats, pork is the most widely consumed in Germany. Braised pork hock (schweinshaxe) and pork stomach (saumagen) are two of Germany's favorite dishes.

On the subject of sausage, the bratwurst may be the most famous food Germany has to offer. The nation is also rather fond of cabbage, turnips, and beets in its meals. Potatoes and sauerkraut are also immensely popular staples of the German cuisine, as well as cuisines of the world over.

The most popular alcoholic beverage in Germany is undoubtedly beer, and the nation serves as a home to lots of different varieties of the drink. Yes! The Germans love their beer about as much as life itself in some cases. Some of the varieties of beer that Germany has produced are Pilsner, Weizenbier, and Alt, all of which were originally made in ordinance with 'purity law' of 16th century Bavaria that mandated brews to be made only with hops, barley, and water. Schnapps and Brandy are also very popular in Germany.

Art
When one thinks of artistic contributions made on German soil, composers are usually the first people who come to mind. Beethoven, Bach, and Mozart (even though he was Austrian) immediately pop into anyone's head. And perhaps the classical music buff even recalls the works of Schoenberg, Alban Berg, and the other late composers of The Second Viennese School. When all of these giants are considered, it becomes more obvious that many believe that it was Germany who dominated most stages of classical music, but Germany's artistic output is not limited just to music.

Workforce
Germany, with its stolid value placed on precision and detail, has gained quite a reputation as a great home to highly skilled engravers and woodcutters. In addition to their contributions to these art forms, they are also known for architectural works of great importance. Their output in architecture has been strong for centuries now, surviving and even thriving throughout the Romanesque, Gothic, Classicist, Baroque, Rococo, and Renaissance periods. These works have taken numerous forms, including cathedrals, public buildings, and even castles. The Brandenburg Gate comes to mind as one of the many examples of the classical German style.

The German desire for orderliness and exactitude invades each and every facet of the life of the nation. This phenomenon is not by any means divorceable from the working life of Germany either, including the business sector. It is widely known among Germans that surprise, humor, or anything even remotely tongue and cheek is not typically welcomed among the businessmen and women of Germany. They are the most pragmatic and conscientious people. Every moment of the waking life of the business class workers are carefully planned and decided upon beforehand. Every moment leads up to the next, with little to no room for variance when it comes to decisions which have already been made.

Engineers are highly esteemed in German culture, and also very well paid at that. This comes as no surprise when considering some of the traits that engineers all have in common: analytical and management skills, attention to detail, and conscientiousness. This is also evidenced clearly by Germany's continuing success in the automotive industry. This nation has lots of respect for hands on expertise, a quality that is usually not very appreciated in the west anymore. This is why professionals with this trait typically do better in the business world of Germany than those who can only boast a financial or educational background.

The German workforce also values diligence and competence over interpersonal skills. This is one trait which Germany shares with most of its western neighbors. The German people are not highly regarded as being very diplomatic or friendly in their speech with coworkers, clients, or other outsiders. They are, above all, direct in these instances.

All traits and factors may culminate to give the impression that the German workforce is a dismal, even dreary entity. There may be some grains of truth in this, as work in Germany is no picnic, but it would not be fair to assert that Germany is much worse than her neighbors when it comes to her workers' wellbeing.

Germany is, in fact, one of the best places to work in here in the western world. A person just needs to become accustomed to the business culture of the nation. Germans may at first seem to foreigners sensible, punctual, reserved, precise, target-oriented, cold, arrogant, obedient, sure of themselves, disciplined, plan-oriented, stiff, unfeeling, authoritative, bureaucratic, direct, professional, self-assured, correct, petty, strong, highly orderly, humorless, reliable, principled, perfectionist, and organized.

These stereotypes may reflect the reality of the culture. They also are rooted in cultural standards which perform their functions on a generalized and abstract level. While they may be bothersome and frustrating at times, they ultimately serve better functions than what meets the eye.

Some of the most important cultural standards which Germany adheres to are as follows:

The task at hand is the religion of the people. It takes precedence over all other things and determines the language and dispositions of all workers. The task at hand should, therefore, be focused on more so than anything else. This includes relationships. Relationships in the business world of Germany take on a subordinate role to work, as they probably should.

German business is widely known for its arguably excessive processes, procedures, rules, and regulations. The businessmen and women of Germany value the application of and adherence to contracts and written agreements very highly. Rigid consequences and sometimes harsh penalties are what those who diverge from the contents of these understandings are met with. This fact highlights at once the importance of mutual obligation and the lack of flexibility and individual determination within the business world of Germany.

Consistency and reliability are minor deities to the German business class. Rule orientation and internalized focus of control also serve important functions within the happenings of the German business world. With so much emphasis placed on the importance of structure and order, it comes as no surprise to us to learn that Germans are never open to welcome uncertainty. They therefore prefer binding rules and agreements to curtail any chances of being caught off guard.

German punctuality is also impressive in its widespread application and quotidian adherence. Meetings and appointments are strictly planned, and their times are met with promptitude and certainty. They follow their schedules tightly to ensure certainty in dealing with one another.

With all these constrictions and rigid regulations, it becomes of the utmost importance to separate the private sphere of regular life with the public sphere of business life. The culture just doesn't allow for as much personality to merge between the two. It would make personal life too austere and professional life too free. With this being said, there is made very little room for friendship within the business world of Germany. This is one of the reasons why German workers often get the reputation of being unfriendly and aloof among their foreign coworkers.

And finally, the last point that should be made on the subject of German business is that of the directness of communication within the German business world. Germanic speech is known for being very direct to the point, without any 'dressing' or sugar coating of any sort. This has lots of practical advantages, making language much more explicit and useful, but it can also give off the impression of coldness and unfriendliness. This is just another example of the unique cultural standards of Germany though. And, as with others, it has its merits and demerits alike.

Holidays and Celebrations
Germany, being a predominantly Christian nation, celebrates many of the same holidays that other Christian nations in the west usually do, including Christmas, Easter, and Good Friday. There are also a few holidays and celebrations unique to German culture, including German Unification Day on October 3rd, a recent holiday celebrating

the unification of post war East and West Germany.

The longest, and perhaps most famous, of all German celebrations is Oktoberfest. This festival starts on a specific Saturday in September and ends 16 to 18 days later on the first Sunday of October. This is a celebration marked with and known for lots of drunken revelry and jollity. It started in the year 1810 with a massive celebration of the marriage between Ludwig of Bavaria and Therese Von Sachsen Hildburghausen.

Chapter 4: Finding native speakers to increase your overall understanding of the language and culture

Much like learning a first language, learning a second one takes lots of practice and time. It is rather hard to imagine learning a first language while remaining taciturn around speakers of that language, so why would a student restrain his or her self to silence in the process of learning any language beyond that? It hits all the bull's eye on all the wrong targets to learn a second language without using it for communication, after all, what else is language good for? Learning and speaking a second language also provides opportunity to learn about other cultures from people with potential first-hand experience with the given culture, German in this case. The benefits of practicing a foreign language far outweigh the costs under virtually any given circumstances.

Speaking a foreign language with others can streamline so much of the learning process. It can undermine so much of the complexity and nuance involved in language acquisition, and in a way that won't jeopardize educational value or accuracy, depending on the person being spoken to. Even speaking with one person who knows German or any other foreign language can expose the student to the entirety of that person's vernacular. The speech can be absorbed and digested naturally. The zone of proximal development, a zone discovered by Piaget in which children are naturally given just a little bit more information that they can fully understand, also applies to people learning a second language. It is really just like any other skill in the sense that it really takes practice and patience to develop.

One important reason why communicating using the second language with others works is the complexity of grammatical forms in virtually any language. This makes it difficult or even impossible to fully learn a language. In fact, linguists have not yet been able to fully describe all the grammatical constructs of even a single language. While speaking with another person may not completely run off grammatical difficulties, it can curtail some of the more embarrassing mistakes that can be made. It could also be added that learning from a native speaker can imbue the student with some of the education that the speaker has received, in a way giving the student a formal education by proxy.

While constant studying effort and rote memorization are important factors in learning a new language, the two take on subordinate roles to what is said to the student and what the student reads. These two are the most important factors in new language acquisition. They work together to supply a more useful comprehensible input than other methods of learning do. As the student receives more and more comprehensible input through reading and listening to the language, it becomes easier and easier to absorb more of the vocabulary and grammar of the second language. It creates a self-sustaining positive feedback loop that can end in fluency easier than the average learner expects.

When learning a new language, it is important not to fluster oneself. Studies have on occasion shown that memorizing vocabulary and intensive grammar study are of limited value when compared to other methods of learning. Again, the importance of comprehensive input becomes so clear here. Students in classes more oriented towards comprehensive input than traditional grammar-based classes do better on communication, and even grammar-based tests across the board. These students get the benefits of a learning experience closer to natural education and can easily apply their skills on their own and in the world. In addition, they are even more likely to continue to study foreign languages.

Comprehensive input also plays a major role (if not, the main role) in vocabulary expansion of any language learned. Many multilinguals build up, as the reader can already guess, enormous vocabularies in each and every language that they learn. These huge collections of verbiage have a tendency to accumulate and expand on top of themselves with the passage of time. But this is seldom done with rote vocabulary memorization. These collections of words are almost always the result of comprehensive input over time. Reading is, of course, always important here as well. One study actually showed that people who spoke Spanish as a second language and also happened to read avidly in fact accumulated larger Spanish vocabularies than native Spanish speakers who did not read often.

Whenever a student learns a second language, it is only natural that he or she will tend to be taciturn at times during the beginning stages. These 'quiet periods' are a useful and protective tool in learning, and are typically more common in children, though adults experiencing these should not feel discouraged for doing so. Also, there are no comprehensive input teaching methods which require their students to speak the languages. It is ultimately not very relevant whether or not the student speaks the language openly, although pronunciation could be a hurdle in speaking with others.

The forcing of students to speak when they are not comfortable doing so not only makes them uncomfortable, but it also does virtually nothing for new language acquisition. The ability to speak the language in itself is a result of comprehensive input. A student can avoid learning a new language through trial and error by speaking it as he or she had to do with the first language that he or she had learned. This will bring no setbacks and can even help the student in the learning process.

Speaking with people in German can seem intimidating, out of social apprehension or fear of embarrassment, but there are many ways to get around these barriers that are destructive in language learning. One way, maybe the easiest or the most useful, to circumnavigate these problems is to text people in German. This is one practice which can be especially helpful for those who don't live in German speaking nations and who may not live around very many others who speak German. It cuts distances to nothing and makes communication all the more approachable and accessible.
HelloTalk is a new app and website which provides a great service for those wishing to connect with people across different languages.

Meeting new German speaking buddies is fast and easy as this website is designed for learners aiming to set up new language exchanges.

Meeting native German speakers on this website is very simple. Most, if not all, the users of this website are incredibly enthusiastic and dedicated, so it is to be expected that a student will find people who will help and motivate him or her and expand horizons for the both of them. It is much like many forms of social media, the user can search for other language learners' information to find (in this case) native German speakers, or the user can submit his or her own information and wait to be found by another language learner.

German is just one of over 100 different language options on this website, so any user wishing to find speakers of any other language will have plenty of options. It is all completely free to send messages, make phone calls, or engage in any other forms of communication through this website, so connecting with the German speaking world is almost as easy here as it is in German speaking Europe.

If the idea of phone calls or verbal communication in German fills you with reticence, then HelloTalk is a great app for you to download. This app will read whatever text you submit to it aloud in German with the correct pronunciation used. This is especially useful in getting an idea of the flow of the language and, of course, the pronunciation of its words.

Another great feature that this app has to offer is a feature in which you can say whatever words or phrases into the microphone of your computer and it will type whatever is said back to you in German or another language of your choice. This app will even go so far as to correct your spelling and grammar along the way. If you are ever at a loss as far as translations to or from German are concerned, this app can be a very useful resource to you.

Another useful (and somewhat fun) method to use when learning German with native speakers is the practice of alternating between

German and English. If slots of time are divided up between the two languages, let us say 10-20 minutes for example, greater results can typically be produced. The speakers won't be as fatigued by longer slots of time and they will have an easier time focusing on the languages spoken. As was mentioned before, it is always beneficial to study in shorter periods of time to consolidate memories more effectively. On the other hand, it is also beneficial to increase the amount of time spoken incrementally each day or so to build endurance and skill in speaking the language.

While this strategy may be only for the outgoing and the less timid among us, it is still a very useful one at that. Speaking to strangers can be one of the more exciting and novel means of learning a new language. Conversely though, this can also be a great method for those who are shy as well. The greatest thing about speaking with strangers is that strangers have no idea who you are and most of them will never see you twice. This is great for people with social anxiety surrounding speaking a foreign language because it takes so much pressure off the speaker. As an added bonus, this is a great way to potentially make new friends as people are often very charmed by seeing a non-native speaker trying to tackle such a complex and nuanced language.

One aspect of learning a new language is the inevitable accent disparity that is bound to come up in speaking. This is not something which should be a concern by the student though. It is nearly impossible to master an accent typical of a foreign tongue. Most can't even master their own regional accent and have practically no reason for doing so. While it is natural to be self-conscious of how one sounds to others, especially when speaking a second or third language, it is not always rational to place too much emphasis on this. Most people will either not notice a foreign accent, or not pay much attention to it. What is always more important is that the content is understandable and relatively clear. Other than that, it becomes important not to terrorize oneself into silence.

Circumlocution is a great skill to use in learning a new language. This is also a skill that would be beneficial to use in one's native language as well. It is not always practical to search for direct translations of every single word when learning the vocabulary of a new language. It can be somewhat tedious. If words are navigated towards the use of context and comparison then not only can communication be made easier, but new pathways can be formed by the use of the connections made. It is like thinking in of itself, it is better to know *how* to think than to know *what* to think. Navigating through content towards the appropriate words in a given situation can help the learner to develop skills in language learning in the future.

The hardest part of speaking to someone in a second or third language is always the beginning. This is the case in learning any language period. But it is important to remember that this small apprenticeship does not last forever, and that once something close to fluency is established, it will be retained in the mind with less effort than it took to absorb. The most important thing here is, as always, persistence. While learning with another may initially be intimidating and difficult, it is the offer of a delayed reward which should keep the learner in the game. It is not hard at all to give up here and sometimes extremely hard to stick to studying, so persistence, again, remains of paramount importance.

Chapter 5: How to beat the most difficult part of learning the German language

The beginning stages

It is possible and feasible to learn the German language quickly. The most difficult parts, however, are the beginning stages. Once these stages have been completed, the learning curve increases dramatically, but first it is necessary to cross the first few humps in learning German. These can be beset on every side by pitfalls and mistakes just waiting to be made by the new language learner, which is why it is important to remain cognizant of all facets of the language at hand, and to consider practicing with others for additional editing and advice.

Regardless of your reasons for learning German, whether you have German-speaking friends or relatives, or have been drawn in by the famously strange and intimidatingly long words of the language, it still remains possible to learn the language at your own pace and on your own time.

The freedom to learn this language on your own time, however, comes with responsibility. It still remains important to study persistently in these initial stages, erring on the side of brevity, but also remaining thorough in your study of the language. The utility of speaking the language with friends, acquaintances, and strangers, as well as one website have all been mentioned before. There are, however, other means of learning the language which are equally practical and accessible in which should be mentioned here:

Audio courses, CD programs, and online radio
Internet-based games, and grammar books
Tablet and smartphone apps
German language movies and TV shows
German language books, magazines, and newspapers
Immersion and getting involved with the culture

Again, HelloTalk and other apps and websites like it are also great resources in learning the language. Here you can connect with native German speakers, as well as other language learners, 24/7 for free. This may prove to be more beneficial than any of the resources mentioned above due to the opportunity to connect with others through the language.

One aspect of the German language that is very beneficial to the native English speaker wishing to learn German is that the German language is very closely related to English. This can prove to be very much a head start in the acquisition of the new language. This is also especially important in the initial stages of learning the German language. If vocabulary and grammar of the German language are studied for virtually any period of time, any given English speaker will be able to draw parallels between the two languages with ease. This makes connection forming and inference patterns much easier for the learner to develop. Some native speaker of a language from a different family—a native Japanese speaker for instance—would have a much more difficult time learning German or any other Germanic language than a native English speaker would.

One of the most difficult things for any speaker learning German, however, is Germanic grammar. The main thing that differentiates Germanic grammar from the grammar of lots of other languages is the fact that it seldom changes a large chunk. If not all, most of the grammatical structure which belongs to the German language dates back to the fully inflected modes of the language's ancestry. This grammar is very similar to that of Latin, Greek, and old Russian.

One aspect of this grammar that is incredibly dissimilar to English grammar is sentence structure. Sentences in German are structured in completely different ways than they are in English. This makes parallel or word by word translations of full sentences either ill-advised, or simply impossible, which is just one of the innumerable reasons why the power of inference is so important in learning German or any other language, for that matter. One example of these differences could be: 'someone help me' would turn into 'Jemand hilf mir', which would literally turn into 'someone me help' in English.

As you can see, the grammatical side of the German language is probably the most difficult aspect of the language from a native English speakers' point of view. However, as with all other facets of learning this language, once the ropes have been shown to the learner it becomes much easier to navigate through speaking the language.

It would now prove useful to include a few important first steps in learning this language. These are as follows:

Master the alphabet

The best first step that a student can make in learning a foreign language is pouring over the language's alphabet and finding the similarities and dissimilarities between that language and the student's native language. It is the letters with umlauts (two dots over them) which should have special attention drawn to them. These change the pronunciation of the letters, and therefore how the entirety of the word sounds. Another quirk in German pronunciation, as in English pronunciation, is the drawing together of two letters to produce sounds much different from the sums of their parts. These are also things to watch out for in the initial stages of learning German.

Learn easy words first

Once the alphabet is mastered, it finally becomes possible to move on to the more entertaining period of learning actual words. These first and easiest words are what are known as 'framework' words by educators because their purpose is to provide a framework for future vocabulary.

It is typical to start with basic words and expressions you would like to say and consider learning them online, as it is the easiest way to do so typically. You can then use whatever application or website you have chosen to continue learning your basics. The greatest starters are typically greetings, such as yes, no, please, thank you, sorry, and excuse me.

One website particularly useful in learning the basics is FluentU. This is a website that takes real life videos, such as movie trailers, music videos, inspirational talks, and news, and turns all of the content into German language learning lessons. This service is not limited simply to German though. It takes on all of the world languages that most language learning applications usually do.

Study nouns, adjectives, and verbs

Once some basics have been picked up, it becomes very important to supplement your new knowledge with study of basic nouns, adjectives, and verbs. These are the building blocks of language which everything else is founded upon. Once there has been a framework of some fundamental words and expressions established, there can be more and more built upon it. The words best suited for day to day use are best to learn throughout this period. Some examples are listed below:

Woche, week; *Jahr,* year; *Huete,* today; *Morgen,* tomorrow; *Gestern,* yesterday; *Kalender,* calendar; *Sekunde,* second; *Stunde,* hour; *Minute,* minute; *Uhr,* o'clock; *uhr,* clock; *Können,* can; *Benutzen,* use; *Machen,* do; *Gehen,* go; *Kommen,* come; *lachen,* laugh; *Machen,* make; *Sehen,* see; *Weit,* far; *Klein,* small; *Gut,* good; *Schön,* beautiful; *Hässlich,* ugly; *Schwierig,* difficult.

Come to understand the construction of sentences

The next step in the learning of the language is developing skills in regard to sentence structure. It is beneficial to the learner that most will understand the information construed with or without proper sentence structure, but this nevertheless remains one of the most important aspects of learning any language. Compared to English, German has more options and intricacies in the structuring of sentences, some of which will not be listed here:

The sentence 'I am giving the cat a mouse' would, for instance, translate into *'Ich gebe die Mauze zur Katze'* in German. *Katze* would be in the dative mode here, while *Mauze* would be in the accusative. It is sometimes easy to struggle in remembering which prepositions are in the dative or accusative modes, but there is also some good news for those who have difficulty with this: at certain times, such as this one, it is possible to omit the preposition of a sentence altogether and still retain the ability to clearly express the intention of the sentence by use of its word order and proper noun cases.

Without the preposition of *zur (zu+der)*, the sentence could be written as follows:

Ich gebe der Katze die Maus. (*Maus* is accusative, *Katze* is dative.)

Or with a pronoun:

Ich gebe ihr die Maus. (*Maus* is accusative, *Ihr* is dative.)

Ich gebe sie der Katze. (*Katze is* dative, *Sie* is accusative.)

The following rules would be advantageous to keep in mind when positioning a dative and accusative object within a sentence:
- Dative objects forever and always come before accusative objects.
- If the accusative object is a pronoun, however, it will always be placed before any dative objects.

It is always essential to apply these rules with the correct grammatical case endings. It will often help in avoiding misconstrued sentences, such as *Ich gebe der Maus die Katze.* Unless, of course, you really did mean to say that you wanted to give the cat to the mouse.

A few more examples would be:
Gib dem Hasen die Karotte. (Give the bunny the carrot.)
Gib ihr die Karotte. (Give her the carrot.)
Gib es ihr. (Give it to her.)

Starting to learn simple German phrases

Once word order, along with sentence structure, has been learned the next step in the process of learning German would be to start learning basic phrases. Just as was done with simple words, it is useful to start with phrases that the learner would use on a day to day basis.

Watch German language movies

This one is not only useful, but it is also fun. Once a basic understanding of German has been established, one thing to do with movies that you have already seen would be to watch German dubbed versions of them. And, of course, you could also watch new German language movies. It could be helpful to turn on English subtitles while doing this though, as it may prove difficult to follow along with the speech of the films. As you increase and expand on your German speaking skills movie watching can become easier and easier with the passage of time.

As your comprehension level improves, you could even consider watching German language movies with their original German subtitles. This would be a very interactive method to use as it would almost be like seeing German speaking reality unfold with German subtitles included. A great technique for language immersion. Some of the greatest movies Germany has to offer for these purposes are Sonnenallee, Die Legende von Paul und Paula, Der Baader Meinhof Komplex, Die Fette Jahren sind Vorbei, and Joschka und Herr Fischer.

Reading German language news

This one will not only familiarize you with the language of Germany, but also its happenings and culture. This is a particularly great method for use by students who like politics or knowing about world happenings. In addition, it is also great for picking up vocabulary, as new words can always be highlighted and looked up whenever they come up.

Connecting with German language speakers

This one is another extremely important one that has already been touched on in some detail. In addition to the websites previously listed that offer services for doing this, Meetup.com and Craigslist.org are also easy places to meet native German speakers or even other German learners. These websites have active and diligent learners who can be of great help to practice your German speaking skills with. Making connections with these people can also become a great source of accountability and motivation. Similar sites are numerous and can also be used to meet other learners. One of the greatest things about these websites is that you never know who you will make a connection with.

Modernity offers lots of other unusual resources in language learning in addition to the more traditional methods listed above. It can be helpful in learning a new language to weigh as many options as possible because it is never quite clear what route is going to lead to the most rewarding means of educating oneself. Some of these newer methods of foreign language learning are listed below:

Listening to podcasts in German

There are some podcasts out there with the specific purpose of learning the German language. These are especially useful because unlike other language learning resources these can be used anywhere and at any time. One other aspect of this means of learning German to be noted is their entertainment value. Podcasts are always a more immersive and fun experience than reading language learning books. They can also help with pronunciation, as the learner gets German audio, rather than just text.

There are, of course, many other ways to introduce oneself to German language learning, but the ones listed above should provide a decent starting point for any student looking to get his or her feet wet.

Chapter 6: Learning German in a more formal classroom environment

The German language is one language that increasingly taught at schools all across the world. Most instructional courses on German are within public and private schools and are intended for school aged children and adolescents. There are, however, many German courses intended for the adult looking for further study of the language. In addition, there are many independent tutors available in most cities where German is at all spoken.

Most of these independent courses have enrollment rates ranging from $150-$300 depending on what city they take place in. The hours per week that the classes require are not very extensive or demanding, ranging from 1-10. The overall duration of these courses is, also, not very extensive, ranging from 1-50 weeks usually. The courses are usually for participants aged 18 and up, so it is not typical that the average student will get very many lazy or otherwise bothersome classmates.

The increased opportunity to learn among peers and develop skills with the help of others is probably the best thing that learning German in a classroom setting has to offer. Teachers of these classes usually assign projects to complete with other students in groups. There is opportunity to learn with your peers as well as independently in most classes offered, which gives this method of learning a huge advantage over others which only offer independent or group study. It is like learning a new language itself, sometimes the learner is working with others on developing skills, and most of the time he or she is working independently. The only difference in a classroom setting is that the subject matter is being worked through by a professional instructor, which alleviates so much of the pressure that any given learner has to live with.

These classes, when tailored towards adults, are somewhat like college courses. The workload is typically somewhat robust, though seldom very overwhelming, it is not a very intimate group of classmates, though typically a functional one, and it is usually bereft of the gossip and the bad studentry typical of middle and high schools. It provides a more thorough educational experience mainly because of the fact that students are somewhat obligated to study the material at hand and are more motivated to do so due to their spending of entrance fees. These classes are also beneficial in that students are quizzed and tested here, occurrences that most students would probably not undertake throughout independent study.

Another important element of the classroom learning of German is the ease of the time allotments. Each student agrees to meet at whatever scheduled times there are throughout the week, which makes setting the time aside so much easier. This is also helpful because of the necessity of meeting the schedule. There is added pressure in sticking to a schedule that you as well as others have agreed upon. You are, in a way, made responsible for the successes or the failures of your classmates when you enter one of these classes. One student's absence or poor performance truly can jeopardize the performance of the whole. Foreign language classes are especially beneficial for those who have a hard time keeping and maintaining schedules for this reason.

Another thing preferable about classroom German learning is the motivation an instructor can instill in a student. It becomes so much easier to learn effectively when there is a professional behind you at every step of the process. It gives a learner so much assurance to know that they are relatively safe from any misinformation or bad advice. At the same time, it increases accountability for the learner. He or she becomes responsible for exam scores and homework completion, which in a way enumerates the comprehensive input that the learner is exposed to.

Many German courses independent of formal educational institutions tend to be very student oriented with great student to instructor ratios. The small class sizes tend to make learning much easier and more enjoyable for the average student. It is not uncommon for the instructors of these classes to be able to give all the students one on one attention every day of study.

Conclusion

Congratulations on making it to the end of *Learning German*. Let us hope you have found this book to be both informative and helpful. Let us also hope that all the objectives mentioned in the introduction have met your standards. Now that you have finished this book, it would be useful to apply the skills learned here to any other further practice of the language in the future. There are, as has been mentioned before, many other learning resources out there on this subject available for download or physical purchase.

The next step in your education would be to utilize these resources and find which ones work and don't work for you. The names of multiple websites and apps, most of them free, have been mentioned within this book and there are also many paper materials on the markets useful in learning German.

It is a notable fact that complex tasks have a much higher completion rate when compartmentalized into more digestible parts than when they are left as the big hydras that they start out as. This is useful to know in learning German, and with this information the contents of this book can be made more accessible and serve greater utility to the reader.

Once the initial stages of learning the German language listed in this book have been surpassed, it at once becomes much easier to continue learning. Learning at this stage also becomes more effective and vocabulary and grammar skills work on top of one another to make fluency a reality, eventually and with practice. As in the case of developing any other skill, the learning of German takes, above all, practice and persistence. It is ultimately those who stick with the study the longest and the hardest who get the best results in the end.

German Phrases

A Complete Guide With The Most Useful German Language Phrases While Traveling

© **Copyright 2018 by Dave Smith - All rights reserved.**

The following eBook is reproduced below with the goal of providing information that is as accurate and reliable as possible. Regardless, purchasing this eBook can be seen as consent to the fact that both the publisher and the author of this book are in no way experts on the topics discussed within and that any recommendations or suggestions that are made herein are for entertainment purposes only. Professionals should be consulted as needed prior to undertaking any of the action endorsed herein.
This declaration is deemed fair and valid by both the American Bar Association and the Committee of Publishers Association and is legally binding throughout the United States.

Furthermore, the transmission, duplication or reproduction of any of the following work including specific information will be considered an illegal act irrespective of if it is done electronically or in print. This extends to creating a secondary or tertiary copy of the work or a recorded copy and is only allowed with an expressed written consent from the Publisher. All additional rights reserved.

The information in the following pages is broadly considered to be truthful and accurate account of facts, and as such any inattention, use or misuse of the information in question by the reader will render any resulting actions solely under their purview. There are no scenarios in which the publisher or the original author of this work can be in any fashion deemed liable for any hardship or damages that may befall them after undertaking information described herein.

Additionally, the information in the following pages is intended only for informational purposes and should thus be thought of as universal. As befitting its nature, it is presented without assurance regarding its prolonged validity or interim quality. Trademarks that are mentioned are done without written consent and can in no way be considered an endorsement from the trademark holder.

Introduction

Ask most people what they would do if money was no object, and almost every time, **travel** will appear in the list. Most of us seem to have a hard-wired desire to visit the places we've read or dreamed about throughout our lives.

Visiting other countries is great for expanding horizons, meeting new people, trying new foods, and promoting cultural understanding. One way of getting the most out of your travel experience is by developing rapport—even to a small extent—with the locals. You will be amazed at how much friendlier and more helpful people are, when you make an attempt to communicate with them in their own language, rather than expecting them to automatically know yours.

English is one of the most widely-studied languages in the world, but that doesn't mean the shopkeepers will be particularly comfortable speaking it. If you're willing to make incompetent and probably amusing attempts to speak German, it will most likely ease their anxiety about attempting to speak English to you. Even though many of them talk to English speakers every day, it's only natural to feel a sense of disadvantage when speaking a language that you're not fluent in. You will find that by making yourself vulnerable first, they will more likely go the extra mile to help you.

While it's unlikely you'll be able to learn the whole language before you go, you can learn some key phrases that you should be able to utilize to impress your traveling companions as well as the people you meet—who will hopefully become friends. As well as the basic phrases, this book also offers some basic grammar to help you understand how the phrases are put together. It will teach you pronouns, basic verb conjugation, case, gender, tense, and the fundamentals of sentence structure, such as when word order is reversed, when verbs are moved to the end, etc. Once you have a feel for the basics, you can begin adding the vocabulary. Once you have some vocabulary, it will be easier for you to start recognizing words and phrases in the conversations going on around you; at that point, your ability to learn the language will begin to grow exponentially.

Each phrase is accompanied by a pronunciation guide that should help you wrap your tongue around the words. Keep in mind that very few sounds translate exactly from one language to another. You will not, at first, be able to pronounce German words like a native speaker would, and of course, this will be awkward for you and probably amusing for your hosts and new friends. This is only natural and something every language learner goes through. But if you listen carefully to native speakers and ask for their help, you can develop the ability to approximate the sounds of German to a large degree.

Chapter 1: Visiting Germany (and Other German-Speaking Countries)

Germany, Austria and Switzerland are beautiful places and lots of fun to visit. No matter what time of year you go, there are many fascinating possibilities for entertainment and sightseeing. Check out the many resources on the web for lists of the many places you'll want to visit. And your trip will be greatly enhanced if you can make some friends while you're there.

Whether you're heading to Germany for a gorgeous river cruise on the Rhine, planning on a rousing Oktoberfest party, skiing in the Alps or attending the Frankfurt Book Fair, you can enhance your trip drastically if you find ways to immerse yourself in the culture, including the language.

It isn't necessary to become fluent in German before packing your bags. As a matter of fact, every German student studies English, and even if they aren't comfortable practicing it in front of a native speaker, many of them will be able to communicate with you on some level, especially if you show them that you're willing to make an effort.

Even if you're not fluent (or particularly conversant), it goes a long way if you make an attempt to talk to people in their own language. At the very least, they will feel less ridiculous speaking in halting English if you're reciprocating, by putting your new ability in German on display. Being able to laugh at your own mistakes will make them feel better about theirs, and they are more likely to go the extra step to try to help you. It also shows respect for their culture and demonstrates your willingness to make an effort to connect with them. If you can use some basic German, there is less of a chance of being cheated by deceitful tourist traps!

While it's not possible to learn any language in a few days, it will certainly speed up your efforts if you understand some of the basics of the German language, especially in the ways it differs from English. You can learn phrases and practice them with the people you meet, but without understanding the mechanics of the language, you won't retain them well or be able to use them to make other sentences and grow your language skills. This book will teach you the basic things you need to know to begin building sentences. You will learn noun cases, pronouns, articles and adjectives, verb conjugation, and tenses. Once you have a basic knowledge of the language, you can begin to plug in vocabulary and fine tune your sentence-building skills.

If you happen to be spending time in a country where you can immerse yourself in German, you can become conversant to at least a moderate degree in a surprisingly short time. Listen as much as you can, ask questions about things that you don't understand, and read everything—from billboards to receipts. It's amazing how fast you will begin to recognize words, phrases, grammar points and sentence structure. And you will find that the natives, once they know you are determined to learn, will take a great amount of pleasure in coaching you!

Following is a short primer on German pronunciation and the fundamentals of German grammar, so that you can begin to get a feel for how the language works.

Chapter 2: A Word About Pronunciation

For the most part, there are only a few rules you will need to learn to be able to work out the pronunciation of German words to a moderately acceptable level.

Short versus Long Vowels

In English we have the concept of "short" and "long" vowels, but that description has very little to do with the way the letter is actually pronounced. Have you ever wondered why the "E" in "bed" is called "short," while the e in "heel" is called "long"? Those words have very little to do with describing the sounds of the vowels.
Not so in most other languages. While the rules for when a vowel is long or short are similar (mostly to do with following other vowels), the pronunciation is much more logical than in English. Short "A" for example, is pronounced "ah." Long "A" is pronounced "aah." Simple, right?

It is actually quite intuitive, once you understand the basics. Of course there are exceptions. In German, the same as in English, there are words that have been borrowed from other languages, so the pronunciation does not necessarily match the spelling conventions of the language. That is unfortunately unavoidable, and something you will have to deal with no matter which language you study. Take heart, though, knowing that English is probably the hardest language to learn in that respect, and you've already mastered that one!
Here are the basic sounds of the German language:

Vowel sounds

a – pronounced "ah" in almost every instance
ä – pronounced ĕ, or "eh"
e – pronounced "ay" when long, ĕ or ə when short. An e at the end of a word is almost always voiced, usually by ə, a simple, unstressed short ĕ sound.

i – pronounced ĭ, like "pit," when short, "ee" when long
o – pronounced "oh"
ö – there is not an English equivalent; it's closest to the "I" in "girl" but you make your lips more rounded
u – pronounced "oo"
ű – "oo" but more exaggerated. To approximate it, say "ee" and then push your lips forward.
y – not usually a vowel, except in certain foreign words. In those words (like "typisch") it's pronounced like "oo" but with very rounded lips.

Diphthongs

(two letters combined to make a "single" sound)
au – pronounced "ow"
äu – pronounced "oy"
eu – also pronounced "oy"
ei – pronounced like "eye"
ie – pronounced "ee"

Consonants

(Most are the same as in English, with the following exceptions)
b – At the closing off of a word or in front of a silent consonant it is voiceless (like the English "P").
c – "C" is very rarely found by itself in German, and most of the time it is, or is found at the beginning of a word, it has been imported from another language. While in those words it's generally pronounced as it is in the foreign words, in certain cases it's pronounced like the beginning sound of "tsar," in others like "chain." There isn't an actual rule here. You just have to know the words.
d – At the closing off of a word or in front of a silent consonant it is voiceless (like the English "T").
g – It's hard, like "gold," except at the closing off of a word or in front of a silent consonant, when it is voiceless (like the English "K").
qu – Pronounced "kv"
s – At the beginning of a word it's pronounced "v" unless it's paired with a voiceless consonant. Whenever it's with a voiceless consonant

it is pronounced "sh."
v – Always voiceless, like the English "F"
w – Pronounced "v"
z – Pronounced "ts"
β – This substitutes for "ss" after a long vowel or a diphthong (except in Switzerland, where they write out the "ss"). It doesn't affect the pronunciation; it's just a writing convention.
ch – This is an odd one. It is roughly pronounced "sh," but when you say it, bring your tongue slightly upward and forward and pull your lips back a bit, keeping them slightly rounded. It sounds a bit like a cat hissing, but the "s" is softer. It takes a bit of practice to get this sound right, but don't worry too much about it—it's pronounced differently in different parts of the German-speaking world, and differently again in other Germanic languages like Dutch, where it is considerably harder. For pronunciation, we will use "kh" to signify this sound.

Chapter 3: Nouns, Cases and Gender— Oh, my!

Cases

This is a good time to discuss this case. In English we aren't used to talking about noun cases, because our cases are simplified to the point they are just taught as a variation of the word without much explanation. For example, as a child you are taught to say "I saw him" instead of "I saw he" or "me saw him." This is simply *the way it is*. We don't usually bother to clarify that "I" and "me" are different cases, although we do learn (and generally forget soon afterwards) that the closest word to being the direct object of the sentence is "me", and so it differs from its subject. It doesn't occur to most of us to wonder why pronouns change when they act as direct objects but other nouns do not. We're also taught that possessives require special treatment, and that also becomes just *the way it is*. But when we learn possessives like "my car" or "my son's bike" we are also using case, although we tend not to think of it that way.

German has a much more complicated case system than English does, and most students find this very intimidating. Rightly so, because it is a foreign concept to most of us and requires some work to conquer, but take heart. It is certainly possible to make yourself understood even when your mastery of case endings is not perfect. And it will come easier with time, practice and a little determination.

German has four cases. For simplicity, we'll call the first one the subjective case because it's usually the subject of the sentence. If you go on to study the language in other venues, you will probably see it referred to as the nominative case, but it's easier to remember when you relate "subject" to "subjective." This is the case of the pronoun forms "I," "he/she," "we," or "they." Remember that we're talking mostly about pronouns because that is where case usually shows up in English. Most nouns are no different in the position of subject than direct object: "The cat is on the bed" versus "Have you seen the cat?"

The next case is the objective case, because it's usually the direct object. Again, you will also see that this is called the accusative case, but we will stick with the more descriptive title. This is the case you're using when you say "me," "him/her," "them," or "us." (Many people have confusions with "who" and "whom" because of the traditional insistence that the objective case of "who" to be used, even though it is a dying distinction in English.)

The third case is called the dative, and we don't really use it in English. This is generally used with (or in place of) prepositions. (Think of it as "going ON a date," and it may help.)

Prepositions in German are confusing at best. Of course when you use a preposition it is followed by a noun ("under the table," "around the corner," "through the door"). These nouns in German need to take either the objective or the dative case, depending on the preposition they're being used with, and the only way to remember which is which—is to memorize them. Unfortunately, there's no other logic to it than that.

Here is a list of common prepositions that take the objective case:

without	**ohne**	*ō'-nə*
against, toward	**gegen**	*gā'-gen*
along	**entlang**	*ĕnt-lŏng*
until	**bis**	*bĭs*
around	**um**	*um*
for	**für**	*fyur*
through, across	**durch**	*doorsh*

Here is a list of common prepositions that take the dative case:

from	**aus**	*ous*
except for	**ausser**	*ous'-er*
by, at	**bei**	*bī*
of, from	**von**	*fŏn*
for, since	**seit**	*zīt*
after	**nach**	*nokh*

with	**mit**	*mĭt*
to	**zu**	*tzoo*
opposite	**gegenüber**	*gā-gen-oo-ber*
under	**unter**	*un'-ter*

The fourth case is the easiest to remember: the possessive case. We just think of it as expressing possession, but it is an actual case, even in English, marked by the apostrophe plus s, or the use of "my," "your," "his/her," "their," and "our." If you're wondering how a noun would be possessive without a possessive pronoun, think of it as "of the ___." So, just as in English "the man's wife" could also be expressed as "the wife of the man," in German you could say "der Manns Frau" or "die Frau des Mannes."

Gender

There is one more complicating factor that affects the cases. That is the presence of male, female and "neuter" nouns. This may seem like an obvious and unimportant detail, but keep in mind that all articles, pronouns and adjectives must match the noun's gender and case. In English we only think of gender when it is obvious, and we only mark it for people. While the gender of many nouns is what you'd expect, that is not always the case, and you definitely can't count on it. In German it is perfectly acceptable to speak of a girl as "it" since the German word for girl (das Mädchen) is neuter, but generally you would only do that if you've just used the word Mädchen. Don't stress out too much about that, though. It's also perfectly acceptable (and will probably keep you safer from embarrassment, not to mention brain damage!) to use "she" if you're talking about an actual girl, "he" if you're talking about a masculine cat, and "she" if you're referring to a female dog.

The subjective case is not too difficult to deal with in terms of noun gender. Granted, you will find yourself confused and wracking your brain trying to remember if you've heard "der," "das" or "die" used with the word before, but at least there are only three choices there. Although, when it comes to the other cases, the prospect becomes much more daunting. Learning how to select the dative and possessive versions of an article or pronoun is the bane of many German language learners' existence and much too complicated to expect yourself to conquer in a lesson or two.

The best thing you can do to help yourself with this, is to keep in mind that when you learn a German verb, memorize the article with it so that they are linked in your mind. If you repeat "der Hund" (the dog) rather than simply "Hund," it's much more likely to come to mind later when you need it. Then it'll simply be a matter of figuring out which case you're using and what the ending will be. The most effective technique is to get a good handle on the article and pronoun endings, take a guess at the gender if it isn't obvious, and hope for the best. Don't spend a lot of time doing mental gymnastics trying to fit all of the right endings to your articles, adjectives, and nouns—or else you'll never get through a conversation! Fortunately, most Germans are too polite (and will be too impressed with your valiant efforts) to give you much grief if your endings aren't exactly right. They may smile, and they will almost undoubtedly correct you (they *are* German, after all) but it's almost always in a playful or helpful way. They understand the complexities of their language and for the most part, they'll be sympathetic.

Articles

The main thing you need to know backwards and forwards is articles. While the table looks daunting, it's not too difficult to memorize, and later you'll be using it so much, that it will soon be second nature. It's well worth taking a little time to get a good handle on the case differences and their articles. Once you are familiar with that, it will be much easier to translate it to pronouns and then to adjectives.

Article	Nominative	Objective	Dative	Possessive
the (male)	der	den	dem	des
the (neuter)	das	das	dem	des
the (female)	die	der	der	die
the (plural)	die	die	den	der
a (male)	ein	einen	einem	eines
a (neuter)	ein	ein	einem	eines
a (female)	eine	eine	einer	einer
a (plural)	eine	eine	einen	einer

Notice that the endings of ein-words (indirect articles) are mostly identical to direct article (der/die/das) endings. This is true for every case, except masculine, neuter subjective, and neuter objective. In those cases, there is no ending. This is worth noting, since it will come up again.

Other words that you might see in place of articles are "dies" ("this" or "that") or "welche" (which, what, that, who). The words Der, Die, and Das all share their endings.

Articles are often occasionally used as pronouns (as in "The man that sat in front of me..."). In this case "the" and "that" would both be the subjective definite article ("der"). It's just something worth noting for later.

Pronouns

So, let's move on to German pronouns. The main pronoun cases are shown in the table below. Remember that objective and dative both correspond to the English "me," "him/her," "them," and "us." (Obviously, in English "you" does not change, singular or plural, except in the possessive. Unfortunately, this is not the case in German.) Possessives take the same suffixes as the articles above. If this is a foreign concept to you, take off the "ein" from the indefinite article ("a"). What remains is what will need to be added to the pronoun.

Pronoun	Subjective	Objective	Dative	Possessive
I	ich	mich	mir	mein
you (informal)	du	dich	dir	dein
you (formal)	Sie (always capitalized)	Sie	Ihnen	Ihr
he	er	ihn	ihm	sein
she	sie	sie	ihr	ihr
it	es	es	ihm	sein
we	wir	uns	uns	unser
you (plural)	ihr	euch	euch	euer
they	sie	sie	ihnen	ihrer

Note that there are two forms of singular "you." "Sie" is the formal or polite version. It is used when addressing someone that you would not call by their first name, such as a new acquaintance, an older person, or an authority figure. With family, friends, and children, use the informal "du." When in doubt, follow the lead of the person you are talking to, or listen to how others address each other.

The next things to know are the endings for the possessive case. If this seems confusing, remember that possessives are paired with nouns, and nouns require gender markers. In the same way that you need to determine whether a noun takes "der," "die" or "das," you need to know what to put on the end of your possessive pronoun to agree with the noun.

Possessive Pronouns

Masculine

Masculine noun case:	Subjective	Objective	Dative	Possessive
my	mein	meinen	meinem	meines
your (informal)	dein	deinen	deinem	deines
your (formal)	Sein	Seinen	Seinem	Seines
his	ihr	ihren	ihrem	ihres
her	sein	seinen	seinem	seines
our	unser	unseren	unserem	unseres
your (plural)	euer	euren	eurem	eures
their	ihr	ihren	ihrem	ihres

Feminine

Feminine noun case:	Subjective	Objective	Dative	Possessive
my	meine	meine	meiner	meiner
your (informal)	deine	deine	deiner	deiner
your (formal)	Seine	Seine	Seiner	Seiner
his	ihre	ihre	ihrer	ihrer
her	seine	seine	seiner	seiner
our	unsere	unsere	unserer	unserer
your (plural)	eure	eure	eurer	eurer
their	ihr	ihre	ihrer	ihrer

Neuter

Neuter noun case:	Subjective	Objective	Dative	Possessive
my	mein	mein	meinem	meines
your (informal)	dein	dein	deinem	deines
your (formal)	Sein	Sein	Seinem	Seines
his	ihr	ihr	ihrem	ihres
her	sein	sein	seinem	seines
our	unser	unser	unserem	unseres
your (plural)	euer	euer	eurem	eures
their	ihr	ihr	ihrem	Ihres

Plural

Plural noun case:	Subjective	Objective	Dative	Possessive
my	meine	meine	meinen	meiner
your (informal)	deine	deine	deinen	deiner
your (formal)	Seine	Seine	Seinen	Seiner
his	ihre	ihre	ihren	ihrer
her	seine	seine	seinen	seiner
our	unsere	unsere	unseren	unserer
your (plural)	eure	eure	euren	eurer
their	ihr	ihre	ihren	ihrer

If all of those endings look intimidating, note that they are the same as the endings for the indefinite article "ein." Once you have those memorized, it is easy to apply them to your possessive pronouns.

An important note: there are a few relative pronouns in German that are very handy to know. They are **dessen, deren** and **denen**. They all mean "*whose,*" as in:

"That's the boy *whose* mother works in my office."

Dessen is used for male and neuter nouns and **deren** is used for feminine and plural nouns. In this example you would use **dessen**, referring to "boy," rather than **deren** for "mother."

Denen is used with plurals in the dative case. Remember that the dative case is used with many prepositions, such as "with."

"Those are the boys *with* whom my son plays."

You would use **denen** for this, since "boys" is plural and the "with" calls for a dative pronoun.

Nouns

Nouns in German, as you may or may not know, are always capitalized. This can be helpful to a beginning student because you can see immediately which words in the sentence are nouns, taking out some of the analysis. This is a very simple rule, and once you get used to it, it shouldn't cause you any headaches.

Plurals in German are formed in several possible ways:
- adding an "e" (**"der Hund, die Hunde"**) (the dog)
- adding an "n" (**"die Woche, die Wochen"**) (the week)
- adding "er" (**"das Kind, die Kinder"**) (the child)
- putting an umlaut on the vowel (**"der Baum, die Bäume"**) (the tree)
- changing the vowel and adding a suffix (**"der Zug, die Züge"**) (the train)

German nouns also take an "s" in the possessive case, although they do not use an apostrophe as we do in English. There are a few other instances of nouns changing to match their case, but as a beginning student, it's understandable if you don't have them memorized. That can come later.

There is no substitute for good old memorization when it comes to learning noun genders, but there are a few tips that will help. (Of course, you have to memorize these too, but it will make things easier later!)

Der – When you see words that have the following suffixes, chances are they are masculine:
- -ich
- -us
- -ant
- -ast
- -ismus
- -us
- -ling

Die – When you see words that have the following suffixes, chances are they are feminine:
- -enz/-anz
- -ie
- -ur
- -in
- -keit/-heit
- -schaft
- -tät
- -tion/-sion
- -ung
- -ei
- -in
- -ur

Das – When you see words that have the following suffixes, chances are they are neuter:
- -chen
- -lein
- -um

Common Nouns

afternoon	der Nachmittag	nokh'-mit-tak
baby	das Baby	bā'-bē
bed	das Bett	bet
boy	der Junge	yoong-ə
breakfast	das Frühstück	froo'-shtook
brother	der Bruder	broo'-der
building	das Gebäude	ge-boy'-də
business	das Geschäft	ge-sheft'
car	das Auto	ou'-tō
castle	das Schloss	shlos
cell phone	das Handy	hand-ē
chair	der Stuhl	shtool
child	das Kind	kĭnt
city	die Stadt	shtat
coffee	der Kaffee	kah'-fē
corner	die Ecke	eck-ə
daughter	die Tochter	tokh'-ter
day	der Tag	tak
dinner	das Abendessen	ah'-bend-es-en
doctor	der Doktor	doc-tor
dog	der Hund	hoont
door	die Tür	toor
ear	das Ohr	ōr
eye	das Auge	ou-gə
family	die Familie	fa-mē'-lē
father	der Vater	fa'-ter
food	das Essen	ess-en
friend	der Freund (m), die Freundin (f)	froind, froin'-din
girl	das Mädchen	mād'-shən
hair	das Haar	hahr
hand	die Hand	hont
head	der Kopf	kōpf
hotel	das Hotel	hō-tel
hour	die Stunde	shtun-də
house	das Haus	hous
job	der Beruf	be-roof'
lady	die Dame	do'-mə

leg	das Bein	*bīn*
love	die Liebe	*lē'-bə*
lunch	das Mittagessen	*mĭt-tok'-es-en*
man	der Mann	*mon*
map	die Karte	*kar'-tə*
minute	die Minute	*mĭn-oot'*
money	das Geld	*gelt*
month	der Monat	*mō-not*
morning	der Morgen	*mor'-gen*
mother	die Mutter	*moot'-er*
night	die Nacht	*nokht*
people	das Volk	*folk*
person	die Person	*pair-zōn'*
phone	das Telefon	*tele-fōn'*
present	das Geschenk	*ge-shenk'*
problem	das Problem	*prō-blām'*
question	die Frage	*frah'-gə*
restaurant	das Restaurant	*res-tōr-ont*
road/street	die Straße	*shtrah'-sə*
room	das Zimmer	*tzĭm-mer*
second	der Zweite	*tzvīt*
sister	die Schwester	*shves'-ter*
sky	der Himmel	*hĭm-mel*
son	der Sohn	*zōn*
suitcase	der Koffer	*kof'-ər*
sun	die Sonne	*zō'-nə*
table	der Tisch	*tish*
ticket	die Fahrkarte	*făr'-kar-tə*
time	die Zeit	*tzīt*
town	die Stadt	*shtat*
toy	Spielzeug	*shpēl'-tzoig*
tree	der Baum	*boum*
view	Aussicht	*ous'-zikht*
water	das Wasser	*vas'-ser*
way	der Weg	*vek*
week	die Woche	*vō'-khə*
window	das Fenster	*fen'-ster*
woman	die Frau	*frou*
year	das Jahr	*yahr*

Adjectives

In German as in English, adjectives come before the noun. Since this is the case, as you might expect—but is dreaded to hear, they need to have endings to match the gender and case.

The bad news here is that you need to take one extra thing into consideration before attaching the ending.

The good news is that it's a bit simpler than it sounds. The adjective does not necessarily have to have something tacked on to it.

Where the noun has a "strong" ending ("einem," "dieses," etc.), the adjective does not need a case ending. Only one of the words preceding the noun needs to carry a "strong" ending. So you would say, for example, "Der schwer Koffer" (the heavy suitcase). Here "schwer" does not take an "er" ending, because it's already present in "der." However, you would have to say "Ein schwerer Koffer," since "ein" does not take an ending in the masculine subjective case. That leaves it to the adjective to carry the strong ending and show gender.

Common Adjectives

whole	**ganz**	*gonts*
large, tall	**groß**	*grōs*
good	**gut**	*goot*
new	**neu**	*neu*
first	**erst**	*erst*
long	**lang**	*long*
German	**deutsch**	*doitsh*
small	**klein**	*klīn*
old	**alt**	*ahlt*
high	**hoch**	*hōkh*
simple	**einfach**	*īn'-fokh*
last	**letzte**	*letzt*
same, right away	**gleich**	*glīkh*

possible	**möglich**	mōg'-likh
own	**eigen**	ī'-gen
beautiful	**schön**	shōn
late	**spat**	shpāt
important	**wichtig**	vikh'-tik
young	**jung**	yung

Practice

Let's try putting some of these concepts together. Translate these noun phrases, making sure you take into consideration the gender and number (singular or plural) of the noun as you assign the appropriate article or pronoun to it.

my dog (nominative)
my beautiful baby (objective)
his ear (dative)
this late hour (nominative)
our money (possessive)
the first morning (dative)
a city (nominative)
your telephone (informal, objective)
my leg (dative)
our house (possessive)
this afternoon (nominative)
their brother (objective)
the old building (possessive)
her son (dative)
your car (formal, objective)
the child whose dog (subjective)

Chapter 4: Verbs

German verbs are much more regular than English verbs. This is very good news for the German student (finally, something simple!). We are used to tenses, and fortunately there are many similarities in that area too.

Of course, as in English, the fundamental verb "to be" is not quite regular, so let's start there.

I am	**ich bin**	ikh bin
you are (informal)	**du bist**	doo bist
you are (formal singular and plural)	**Sie sind**	zē sint
he/she/it is	**er/sie/es ist**	air/zē/ess ist
we are	**wir sind**	veer zint
you are (plural informal)	**ihr seid**	eer zīt
they are	**sie sind**	zē sint
I have	**ich habe**	ikh hŏb-ə
you have (informal)	**du hast**	doo host
you have (formal singular and plural)	**Sie haben**	zē hŏ'-ben
he/she/it has	**er/sie/es hat**	air/zē/ess hŏt
we have	**wir haben**	veer hŏ'-ben
you have (plural informal)	**ihr habt**	eer hŏbt
they have	**sie haben**	zē hŏ'-ben

The next most important verb, as in English, is "to have." This is used as an auxiliary (or "helping") verb, much as it is in English, with a few exceptions.

Weak Verbs

This conjugation is very close to "regular" or "weak" verbs. **Kommen** ("to come") is a good example of a weak verb.

I come	**ich komme**	*ikh kōm-ə*
you come (informal)	**du kommst**	*doo kōmst*
you come (formal singular and plural)	**Sie kommen**	*zē kōm-ən*
he/she/it comes	**er/sie/es kommt**	*air/zē/ess kōmt*
we come	**wir kommen**	*veer kōm-ən*
you come (plural informal)	**ihr kommt**	*eer kōmt*
they come	**sie kommen**	*zē kōm-ən*

As you can see, regular conjugation is fairly simple. Most German verbs follow this same pattern:

I: **-e**
you (informal): **-st**
you (formal, singular and plural): **-en**
he/she/it: **-t**
we: **-en**
you (plural, informal): **-t**
they: **-en**

Another regular but important verb is "to go," **gehen**. Here is its conjugation:

I go	**ich gehe**	*ikh gā'-ə*
you go (informal)	**du gehst**	*doo gāst*
you go (formal singular and plural)	**Sie gehen**	*zē gā'-ən*
he/she/it goes	**er/sie/es geht**	*air/zē/ess gāt*
we go	**wir gehen**	*veer gā'-ən*
you go (plural informal)	**ihr geht**	*eer gāt*
they go	**sie gehen**	*zē gā'-ən*

Note: "To go" is used a bit differently in German. In English we might say, "I am going to Frankfurt" but in German you would say "I am traveling (fahren) to Frankfurt."

Here is a breakdown of the traveling verbs that can be confusing:
- **gehen**: go, move, leave, walk, go down, quit
- **fahren**: run, ride, drive, pass, move
- **kommen**: get, reach, come, arrive, go

These verbs have another unique trait, which will be described in the section on past tense. For now, just keep them in mind as a related group.

Then there is **haben** (to have), an extremely important verb.

I have	**ich habe**	*ikh hăb'-ə*
you have (informal)	**du hast**	*doo hăbt*
you have (formal singular and plural)	**Sie haben**	*zē hăb'-ən*
he/she/it has	**er/sie/es hat**	*air/zē/ess hăt*
we have	**wir haben**	*veer hăb'-ən*
you have (plural informal)	**ihr habt**	*eer hăbt*
they have	**sie haben**	*zē hăb'-ən*

Here is a list of common German regular verbs:

to eat	**essen**	*ess-ən*
to go, drive	**fahren**	*fahr'-ən*
to see	**sehen**	*zā-ən*
to want	**wollen**	*vōl'-ən*
to bring	**bringen**	*bring'-ən*
to think	**denken**	*denk'-ən*
to write	**schreiben**	*shrīb'-ən*
to buy	**kaufen**	*kouf'-ən*
to help	**helfen**	*helf'-ən*
to make	**machen**	*mokh'-en*
to drink	**trinken**	*trink'-ən*
to become	**werden**	*vair'-dən*

Strong verbs

Usually, the main difference between strong and weak verbs is that the vowel changes during conjugation in the second and third person singular. There isn't a hard and fast rule about which verbs are strong, and what their vowels will change into, but it's a pretty decent bet that any newly formed verbs (like "surfen") will be weak.
So a word like "**brechen**" (to break) will conjugate in the following way:

Ich breche, du brichst, Sie brechen, er/sie/es bricht, wir brechen, ihr brecht, sie brechen

may, to be allowed	**dürfen**	darf
to eat	**essen**	ißt
to give	**geben**	gibt
to help	**helfen**	hilft
can, to be able to	**können**	kann
to run	**laufen**	läuft
must	**müssen**	muss
to take	**nehmen**	nimmt
to sleep	**schlafen**	schläft
to speak	**sprechen**	spricht
to meet	**treffen**	trifft

There are too many strong verbs to try to memorize, but there are some that it is imperative to know:

One of the biggest differences between English and German when it comes to verbs is the present tense. In English there is a difference between "I am going" and "I go." In German, the present tense ("I go") serves as the simple or progressive present ("I am going"), the habitual present ("I go every Saturday"), and also the future ("I will go" or "I am going to go").

Past Tense

Simple past is most often formed by adding a **-t** at the end of the word, but often the vowel is changed as well. Many of the strong forms were brought over into English so will already be familiar.

Past tense weak verbs are conjugated in the following way:

I said	**ich sagte**	*ikh zăg'-tə*
you said (informal)	**du sagtest**	*doo zăg'-test*
you said (formal singular and plural)	**Sie sagten**	*zē zăg'-tən*
he/she/it said	**er/sie/es sagt**	*air/zē/ess zăgt*
we said	**wir sagten**	*veer zăgt'-ən*
you said (plural informal)	**ihr sagtet**	*eer zăg'-tet*
they said	**sie sagten**	*zē zăg'-ten*

Past tense strong verbs, as you might expect, can be conjugated in several different ways, but for the most part the endings will be pretty close to weak verb endings.

Here are a few examples:

I went	**ich ging**	*ikh gĭng*
you went (informal)	**du gingst**	*doo gĭngst*
you went (formal singular plural)	**Sie gingen**	*zē gĭng'-ən*
he/she/it went	**er/sie/es ging**	*air/zē/ess gĭng*
we went	**wir gingen**	*veer gĭng'-ən*
you went (plural informal)	**ihr gingt**	*eer gĭngt*
they went	**sie gingen**	*zē gĭng'-en*

I spoke	**ich sprach**	*ikh shprakh*
you spoke (informal)	**du sprachst**	*doo shprakhst*
you spoke (formal singular and plural)	**Sie sprachen**	*zē shprakh'-ən*

he/she/it spoke	**er/sie/es sprach**	*air/zē/ess shprakh*
we spoke	**wir sprachen**	*veer shprakh'-ən*
you spoke (plural informal)	**ihr spracht**	*eer shprakht*
they spoke	**sie sprachen**	*zē shprakh'-en*

Present Perfect

In German, as in English, "to have" is used to make the present perfect in most cases ("I have seen"). One important difference is that some German verbs take "to be" as the auxiliary verb for the perfect tenses. "To be" itself, as well as almost all verbs that mean travelling from one place to another, use this form. So you would say "I am been," "they are gone" or "he is driven" instead of "I have been," "they have gone" or "he has driven." This seems odd to English speakers but really does not take long to get used to.

The past participles (used with the auxiliary verbs "have" or "be") are formed in a few different ways. Most add **ge-** to the beginning of the word, some remove the **-n** or **-en** from the end and add **-t**, and some change their vowels or the form of the middle part.

English	*German infinitive*	*Present*	*Simple past*	*Past participle*
to go	**gehen**	**geht**	**gang**	**ist gegehen**
to buy	**kaufen**	**kauft**	**kauft**	**hat gekauft**
to help	**helfen**	**hilft**	**half**	**hat geholfen**
to bring	**bringen**	**bringe**	**bracht**	**hat gebracht**
to know (as in facts)	**wissen**	**weißt**	**wußt**	**hat gewußt**
to eat	**essen**	**ißt**	**aß**	**hat gegessen**
to drive/go	**fahren**	**fährt**	**fuhr**	**ist gefahren**
to stay	**bleiben**	**bleibt**	**blieb**	**ist**

				geblieben
to sleep	**schlafen**	**schläft**	**schlief**	hat geschlafen
to lose	**verlieren**	**verliert**	**verlor**	hat verloren
to drink	**trinken**	**trinkt**	**trank**	hat getrunken
to see	**siehen**	**sieht**	**sah**	hat gesehen
to speak	**sprechen**	**spricht**	**sprach**	hat gesprochen

There is a group of weak (regular) verbs that take the **-t** at the end but not the beginning **ge-**. These are mostly words that end in **-ieren** like **diskutieren** ("discuss").

Past Perfect

As intimidating as this sound, it's going to be the easiest part of the verb discussion. As a refresher from your school days, past perfect is simply a variation on present perfect tense.

Present Perfect: "I *have* seen that movie" (as of this present moment I have seen the movie)
Past Perfect: "I *had* seen that movie" (at some point in the past when the topic came up, I had already seen the movie)

You create the past perfect simply by using the conjugated past tense of "have," exactly as in English.

There are other, more complicated verb tenses, but there's no need to worry about them at this stage of your learning. They are present in English, too, but as with most aspects of language learning, once you learned to use them as a child, you stopped thinking about how to do it. It is only when you try to transfer the concepts to other languages that you have to re-learn the concepts.

Practice
So let's try some conjugating. Remember there are a couple of things to take into consideration, such as changing vowels, past forms, and modal verbs. Take your time and really start to get a feel for how the language works!
we are eating
you (plural, informal) go
I see
she has spoken
they drive
you (formal) see
I have eaten
we had brought
they have gone
it stayed
you (informal) lost
she will buy
they were drinking
we said

Chapter 5: Word Order

Word order differs between German and English in a few ways that may seem quite confusing at first. However, it is fairly logical and not too difficult to master with just a bit of practice.

Sentence Structure
Simple sentences take the same order as English sentences:
"*I see you,*" "*He wants that.*"

The basic order of a sentence is the subject first, the verb second, followed by the indirect object, and finally the direct object.

"*I am giving a treat to the dog.*" (not "I am giving the dog a treat.")

Normal order of a temporal sentence with location is: Time, manner, place

"*Tomorrow we will go by bus to the mountains.*"

Sentences with two parts connected by the conjunctions "and," "or," "but," and "rather" keep the same order as a simple sentence.

"*She got a cat, but I prefer dogs.*"

Auxiliary Verbs (*must, can, should*, etc.)
This is where it begins to sounds strange to English speakers, but it is actually quite easy to get used to. If you use an auxiliary verb (sometimes called a "helping verb"), the second verb in the sentence will take the infinitive form (almost always ending in "-en") and comes at the end.

"*Can you the book on my desk leave?*"

This is also true for the perfect (and past perfect) tense.
"*I have nobody seen.*"

Clauses
<u>Relative clauses</u> (as a refresher, a relative clause can be removed from a sentence without changing its meaning)

In most cases, the verb in a relative clause comes at the end.

"*My brother, who in Denver lives, is coming for Christmas.*"

<u>Subordinate Clauses</u>
"*Because I home stayed, missed I the movie.*"

"Because I stayed home" is a subordinate clause: it cannot stand as a sentence on its own. It is not a relative clause because removing it would change the meaning of the sentence. It would simply be "I missed the movie," without giving the reason.
In German, subordinate clauses are formed by putting the conjunction ("because") first and the verb last. This is a common formation, but when "because," along with a few other select conjunctions (when, if, since, until, that, before, despite, as far as, as soon as, how, while, so that, during, where, as long as) is present, **always** move the verb to the end of a clause.

Notice that when the verb comes at the end of a clause followed by a comma, the next verb is placed immediately following it. This is also known as the "verb comma verb" rule.
"*After she dinner ate, did she the dishes.*"
If the conjunction is in the second clause, the conjugated verb is still moved to the end, but obviously the comma is followed by the conjunction rather than by a verb.
"*I will go to work, as long as I better feel.*"

Verb Inversion
Temporal words at the beginning of a statement cause the verb to be inverted.

"Tomorrow go we to the zoo."

Questions cause the verb to be inverted. Unlike English, auxiliary verbs are not used to create questions.
"Watch you the movie with us?"

Verbs after question words (why, what, who, when, etc.) are inverted, rather than using auxiliary verbs.
"Why said she that?"

Question Words
   Who - **Wer**
   What – **Was**
   Where – **Wo**
   Why – **Warum**
   When – **Wann**

It's not necessary to memorize all of these rules right now. Learning some basic stock phrases will impress your hosts, friends and strangers. But if your aim is to actually begin to learn German, these rules will give you a structure that you can build on as you get a feel for the language and begin to fill in vocabulary and develop your listening skills.

Practice
Let's use the grammar rules and vocabulary you've learned so far to begin to create sentences. Remember, the more familiar you get with the structures now, the easier it will be to memorize the common phrases you'll use while traveling, follow conversations (because you won't spend so much time being confused about words being "in the wrong place"), and actually have conversations when you start developing the skills and vocabulary.

The girl has learned German.
Are you (informal) writing?
We had been drinking coffee.
The child has lost its (gender unknown) money.

The town has an old tree.
Where is my son?
Is this the family of the tall boy?
We drove until afternoon.
My brother bought a new cell phone from your business.
Their sister had seen a woman.
I bought a toy for my child.
Our room has a beautiful view.
Is their map under the table?
Did you meet my beautiful sister?

Chapter 6: Fundamental Vocabulary

Days of the Week

Monday	Montag	mahn'-tahk
Tuesday	Dienstag	deens'-tahk
Wednesday	Mittwoch	mit'-vokh
Thursday	Donnerstag	donners'-takh
Friday	Freitag	frī'-takh
Saturday	Samstag / Sonnabend	zoms'-takh/zōn'-abent
Sunday	Sonntag	zōn'-takh

Months

January	Januar	yah'-nuahr
February	Februar	feb'-ruahr
March	März	mairtz
April	April	ah-pril'
May	Mai	my
June	Juni	yoo'-nee
July	Juli	yoo'-lee
August	August	ow-goast
September	September	zept-em'-ber
October	Oktober	ok-tō'-ber
November	November	nō-vem'-ber
December	Dezember	day-tzem'-ber
monthly	monatlich	mō-naht'-likh
yearly	jährlich	jehr-likh

Time

What time is it?	Wie spät ist es?	vee shpāt ist es
It is...	Es ist...	es ist...
twelve o'clock	zwolf Uhr	tzvölf oor
two-fifteen	zwei Uhr fünfzehn	tzvī oor fuenf'-tzān
three-thirty	drei Uhr dreißig	drī oor drī'-sik
four-forty-five	vier Uhr fünfundvierzig	feer oor fuenf-unt-feer'-tzik
noon	Mittag	mit'-tak
midnight	Mitternacht	mit'-ter-nakht
this morning	heute Morgen	hoy'-ta mor'-gen
tonight	heute Abend	hoy'-ta ah'-bent
today	heute	hoy'-ta
tomorrow	morgen	mor'-gen
yesterday	gestern	gĕ'-stern
last night	letzter Nacht	letz-ter nokht
day after tomorrow	übermorgen	oo'-ber-mor-gen
next week	nächste Woche	nāsh'-ta vō-kha
next month	nächste Monat	nāsh'-ta mö'-not
last week	letzte Woche	letz-ta vō-kha
see you (until)...	bis...	biss

Chapter 7: Basic Phrases

Basic phrases are the fundamental building blocks of everyday language use. With the exceptions of individual letters and words, of course, they are the most important part of learning and speaking any language. Here we will delve into the some of the most common and useful phrases that the German language has to offer.

yes	ja	yah
no	nein	nīn
thank you	danke	dahnk-ə
thank you, too [in reply to "thank you" from someone else]	Ich danke Ihnen auch	ikh donk-ə een'-en oukh
please	bitte	bitt-ə
you're welcome	bitte schön	bit-tə shone
no problem	kein problem	kīn proh-blām'
excuse me; sorry	entschuldigung	ent-shuld'-igung
naturally; of course	natürlich	na-toor'-lish
correct	richtig	rikh'-tik
thank you very much	vielen dank	feel-en donk
no, thank you	nein, danke	nīn donk-ə
sorry (it gives me pain)	es tut mir leid	ess tūt meer līd
forgive me	verzeihen Sie	ver-tzī'-en zee
isn't that right?	nicht wahr	nikht var

Getting to Know You...

This section is comprised of phrases for use in casual conversations within the German vernacular.

(I am called...) My name is	**Ich heiße ...**	*ikh hīs-ə*
(informal) What is your name? (What are you called?)	**Wie heißt du?**	*vee hīst du*
(formal) What is your name?	**Wie heißen Sie?**	*vee hī'-sen zee*
(informal) Where are you from? (From where do you come?)	**Woher kommst du?**	*vo-hair comst du*
(formal) Where are you from? (From where do you come?)	**Woher kommen Sie?**	*vo-hair com'men zee*
I'm from...	**Ich komme aus...**	*ikh comm-ə ous*
(informal) I am happy to meet you.	**Nett dich kennenzulernen.**	*net dish ken'-nen-tzu-lair-nen*
(formal) I am happy to meet you.	**Nett Sie kennenzulernen.**	*nett zee ken'-nen-tzu-lair'nen*
(formal) Could I introduce you to...?	**Darf ich Ihnen ... vorstellen?**	*Darf ikh ee-nen ... for-shtêl-en*
My pleasure.	**Freut mich.**	*froyt mikh*
When is your birthday?	**Wann hast du Geburtstag?**	*von hast doo ge-boorts'-tak*
My birthday is in May.	**Mein Geburtstag ist im Mai.**	*mīn ge-boorts'-tak ist im mī*
(informal) Do you have children?	**Hast du Kinder?**	*hast doo kind'-er*
(formal) Do you have children?	**Habben Sie Kinder?**	*hab'-ben zee kind'-er*
(informal) Where do you live? (Where live you?)	**Wo wohnst du?**	*vō vōnst doo*
(formal) What place do you live at?	**Wo wohnen Sie?**	*vō vōn'-en zee*

My job is X.	**Ich bin X von Beruf.**	*ikh bin x fahn be-roof*
What do you normally do outside of work? (informal)	**Was machst du außerhalb der Arbeit?**	*vos mokhst doo ou-ser-holf dair ar'-bīt*
What are your activities outside of work? (formal)	**Was machen Sie außerhalb der Arbeit?**	*vos mokh-en zee ou-ser-holf dair ar'-bīt*
My hobbies are X, Y, and Z.	**Meine Hobbies sind X, Y, and Z.**	*mīn hobbies zint X, Y, unt Z*
I like to do X.	**Ich mache gerne X.**	*ikh makh-ə gern-ə X*
To get on with	**Auskommen Mit**	*Ows-komen met*
To describe	**Beschreiben**	*Besh-raben*
To go to sleep	**Einschlafen**	*In-Shlafen*
Love	**Liebe**	*Leeb*
To love	**Lieben**	*Leeb-n*
Part	**Teil**	*Tal*
To share	**Teilen**	*Tal-n*
Address	**Adresse**	*Address*
Age	**Alter**	*Al-tr*
Surname	**Brille**	*Bril*
Born	**Geboren**	*Ge-boar-en*
Birth (day/place of)	**Geburts (tag/ ort)**	*Ge-brrts*
Home	**Heimat**	*Ha-mat*
Home journey/ Way home	**Heimfahrt/ Heimweg**	*Ham-fart/ Ham-weg*
To marry	**Heiraten**	*Har-atin*
Single/ Unmarried	**Ledig**	*Lee-dig*
Dear (=letters)	**Leiber/ leibe**	*Librr/ Lib*
Married	**Verheiratet**	*Fer-har-atet*
Engaged	**Verlobt**	*Fer-lobt*
To promise	**Versprechen**	*Fer-spre-kin*
First name	**Vorname**	*For-nam*
Old (fashioned)	**Alt (modisch)**	*Alt (mo-deech)*
Pleasant/ Enjoyable	**Angenehm**	*An-ge-nem*
Famous	**Berhühmt**	*Brr-hoomt*

Small Talk

This section further explores words and phrases useful in getting to know another person in casual conversation.

(informal) How are you? (How does it go with you?)	**Wie geht es dir?**	*vee gāt es deer*
(formal) How are you? (How does it go with you?)	**Wie geht es Ihnen?**	*vee gāt es eenen*
(informal) Do you come here often?	**Kommst du oft hierher?**	*comst du oft here-hair*
(formal) Do you come here often?	**Kommen Sie oft hierher?**	*comen zee oft here-hair*
(informal) Can you speak English?	**Sprichst du Englisch?**	*shprikht du eng'-lish*
(formal) Can you speak English?	**Sprechen Sie Englisch?**	*shprekh-en zee eng'-lish*
I don't speak German (very well).	**Ich kann nicht (gut) Deutsch sprechen.**	*ikh con nikht zo goot doich shprekh'-en*
I can speak only a small amount of German.	**Ich spreche nur ein bisschen Deutsch.**	*ikh shprekh-ə noor īn bish-en doitsh*
I didn't understand.	**Ich verstehe nicht.**	*ikh vairshtay-ə nikht*
(informal) Would you mind repeating that?	**Kannst du das bitte weiderholen?**	*const du doss bitt-ə vee'-derholen*
(formal) Could you please say that again?	**Können Sie das bitte wiederholen?**	*cun'-nen zee doss bitt-ə vee'-der-hol-en*
(informal) Please say that again.	**Bitte, wiederholen.**	*bitt-ə vee'-der-hol-en*
(formal) Please say that again.	**Bitte, wiederholen Sie.**	*bitt-ə vee'-der-hol-en zee*

(informal) Could you please speak a little more slowly?	**Kannst du bitte langsamer sprechen?**	*const doo bitt-ə long'-zahm-er shprek'-en*
(formal) Could you please speak a little more slowly?	**Können Sie bitte langsamer sprechen?**	*cun-nen zee bitt-ə long'-zahm-er shprekh'-en*
What is X called in German?	**Wie heißt X auf Deutsch?**	*vee hīst x ouf doitsh*
How would someone say X in German?	**Wie sagt man X auf Deutsch?**	*vee zakt mon x ouf doitsh*
Would you translate that?	**Können Sie das übersetzen?**	*kun'-nen zee dos oo-ber-zet'-sen*
Thanks a lot for helping!	**Vielen Dank für Ihre Hilfe!**	*feel-en donk fyur eer-ə hilf-ə*
Do you understand? (informal)	**Verstehst du?**	*fair-shtāst doo*
Do you understand? (formal)	**Verstehen Sie?**	*fair-shtā'-en zee*
(informal) Please write that down for me.	**Schreibst du das bitte für mich auf.**	*shrī'-bst doo das bitt-ə fyur mikh ouf*
(formal) Please write that down for me.	**Schreiben Sie das bitte für mich auf.**	*shrī'-ben zee das bitt-ə fyur mikh ouf*
What does that mean?	**Was bedeutet das?**	*vas be-doy-tet das*
I don't know (I know not)	**ich weiß nicht**	*ikh vīs nikht*
all right	**in ordnung**	*in ordnung*
never mind	**macht nichts**	*makht nikhts*
How is the weather?	**Wie ist das Wetter?**	*vee ist dos vet'-er*
see you later	**bis später**	*biss shpāt'-er*
bye	**tschűß**	*shuss*
Take care!	**Machs gut!**	*mokhs goot*
See you!	**Bis dann!**	*bis dăn*
See you later! (Until later)	**Bis später!**	*bis shpāter*

See you soon! (Until soon)	**Bis gleich!**	*bis glīkh*
Get home safe!	**Komm gut nach hause!**	*kom goot nokh houz-ə*
Goodbye!	**Auf Wiedersehen!**	*ouf vee-der-zā'-en*
Have a nice day!	**Einen schönen Tag noch!**	*īn-en shō-nen tok nokh*
Have a good night!	**Gute Nacht!**	*goot-ə nokht*
Have a nice weekend!	**Schönes Wochenende!**	*shō'-nes vōkh'-en-en-də*
See you next time!	**Bis zum nächsten Mal!**	*bis tzoom nākh-sten mol*
Joy	**Freude**	*Froy-d*
Friendly	**Freundlich**	*Froynd-lik*
Awful	**Furchtbar**	*Furkt-bar*
Patient	**Geduldig**	*Ge-dul-dig*
To like	**Gefallen**	*Ge-fallen*
Tall	**Groß**	*Gross*
Size/ height (of a person)	**Größe**	*Grawss*
Helpful	**Hilfsbereit/ Hilfreich**	*Hillfs-berat/ Hill-frak*
Polite	**Höflich**	*Haw-flikh*
Pretty	**Hübsch**	*Hyub-skh*
Small/ short	**Klein**	*Klan*
Clever	**Klug**	*Klug*
Funny	**Komisch**	*Ko-mikh*
In a good/ bad mood	**Laune (Guter/ Schlechter)**	*Lawn (Goo-tr/ Shlekh-r)*
Noisey/ loud	**Laut**	*Lawt*
Curley	**Lockig**	*Lok-ig*
Tired/ tiring	**Müde/ ermüdend**	*Myud/ er-muydn-d*
Nice	**Nett**	*Net*
Tidy	**Ordentlich**	*Orden-likh*
Rich	**Reich**	*Raikh*

Clean	**Sauber**	*Saw-br*
Sharp	**Scharf**	*Sh-arf*
Slim	**Schlank**	*Shl-ank*
Shy	**Schüchtern**	*Shyukh-ern*
Strong	**Stark**	*Stark*
Strict	**Streng**	*Streng*
Sad	**Traurig**	*Traw-rig*
Untidy	**Unordentlich**	*Un-orden-likh*
To understand (get on with)	**Verstehen (sich)**	*Fer-ste-hn (sikh)*

Shopping

This section is comprised of words and phrases that are useful to the native English speaker preparing to shop at any German-speaking establishment.

Some helpful tips for the foreigner shopping in Germany are as follows:

In German-speaking Europe (Germany, Switzerland, and Austria) it is never wise to assume that any given store or restaurant will accept credit and/or debit card payments. The culture prefers and appreciates cash to electronic payment methods.

Price tags in Germany already include the VAT (value-added tax). This includes sales tax, meaning that the price listed is what the buyer actually pays, unlike in America.

German-speaking nations are much more conservative in their shopping hours; in fact, Germany has a *Ladenschlußgesetz* (or store closing law) that prohibits businesses from remaining open for as long as the common store hours in lots of other countries.

In German supermarkets, there are typically far less brands to choose from than there are in American markets. One important thing for any foreigner about to shop for groceries in Germany is to remember to bring his or her own bag, as they are usually not free in German supermarkets.

And lastly, while there are lots of superstores in German-speaking Europe, there also happen to be lots of specialty stores as well. These stores are incredibly useful as their employees have more knowledge and information to provide customers than their counterparts at the superstores.

With that being said, below is a list of useful words and phrases for shopping in German-speaking countries.

What would you like?	**Was möchten Sie?**	*vos mush'-ten zee*
What are you looking for?	**Was suchen Sie?**	*vos zoo'-khen zee*
Do you have...?	**Haben Sie...?**	*hob-ben zee*
Do you have souvenirs?	**Haben Sie Andenken?**	*hob-ben zee on'-denk-en*
Do you sell...?	**Verkaufen Sie...?**	*fair-kouf'-en zee*
Where do I find...?	**Wo finde ich...?**	*vō find-ə ikh*
Where is...?	**Wo ist...?**	*vō ist*
How much does that cost?	**Wie viel kostet das?**	*vee feel costet dos?*
Can I pay cash?	**Kann ich bar bezahlen?**	*con ikh bar betzol'-en*
Do you accept Visa/Mastercard?	**Nehmen Sie Visa/Mastercard?**	*nām'-en zee Visa/Mastercard*
Could I pay for this with a credit card?	**Kann ich mit eine Kreditkarte zahlen?**	*con ikh mit credit-cart'-ə tzahl'-en*
Where can I find a close ATM?	**Wo ist der nächste Geldautomat?**	*vo ist dair nāsht-ə geld'-out-ō-mot*
Can I buy it for X euros?	**Kann ich es für X Euro kaufen?**	*con ikh ess fyoor x oorohz kouf'-en*
Do you have something that costs less?	**Haben Sie etwas Billigeres?**	*hob-ben zee etvas bill'-ə-gər-ess*

Can I have a discount?	**Können Sie mir darauf Rabatt geben?**	*kun-nen zee meer da-rouf ra-bot' gā-ben*
Does that come in a [bigger/smaller] size?	**Haben Sie das in einer [größeren/kleiner] Größe?**	*hob-ben zee doss in īn'-ər [klī'-ner/grōs'-er-en] grōs-ə*
Could you wrap this as a present?	**Können Sie das als Geschenk einpacken?**	*kun-nen zee dos als ge-shenk īn'-pok-en*
What times does the shop [open/close]?	**Um wieviel Uhr [öffnet/schließt] das Geschäft?**	*um vee-feel oor [uf'-net/shleest] doss ge-sheft*
Where can I find the restrooms, please?	**Wo sind die Toiletten, bitte?**	*vo zind dee toil-et'-ten bit-tə*
Suit	**Anzug**	*Ahn-zug*
Bracelet (wristwatch)	**Armband (uhr)**	*Arm-band (uhr)*
Bra	**BH/ Büstenhalter**	*BH/ Byust-n-hahltr*
Blouse	**Bluse**	*Bloos*
Belt	**Gürtel**	*Gyur-tel*
Necklace	**Halskette**	*Hahl-sket*
Handbag	**Handtasche**	*Hand-tash*
Shirt	**Hemd**	*Him-d*
Trousers	**Hose**	*Hoose*
Hat	**Hut**	*Hut*
Jacket	**Jacke**	*Jak*
Dress	**Kleid**	*Klade*
Clothes/ Clothing	**Kleider/ kleidung**	*Klad-r/ kla-dung*
Tie	**Krawatte/ schlips**	*Kra-waat*
Coat	**Mantel**	*Man-tl*
Skirt	**Rock**	*Rock*
Pajamas	**Schlafanzug**	*Shlaf-ahn-zoog*
Shoes	**Schuhe**	*Shoo*
Sock	**Socke**	*Sock*
Boot	**Stiefel**	*Stafl*

Tights	**Strumpfhose**	*Strumpf-hoos*
To carry/ wear	**Tragen**	*Tra-gen*
Underpants	**Unterhose**	*Oontr-hoos*
Underwear	**Unterwäsche**	*Oontr-wowkh*
Towel (bath towel)	**Handtuch (badetuch)**	*Hand-tookh (bade-tookh)*
Radiator	**Heizkörper**	*Haz-Kirp-r*
Comb	**Kamm**	*Kahm*
Wardrobe	**Kleiderschrank**	*Kladr-shrank*
Lamp	**Lampe**	*Lamp*
Microwave	**Mikrowellenherd**	*Mikro-weln-herd*
Soap	**Seife**	*Safe*
Armchair	**Sessel**	*Ses-sl*
Sofa/ settee	**Sofa**	*Sofa*
Stereo system	**Stereoanlage**	*Stereo-an-lag*
Step/ stair	**Stufe**	*Stoof*
Chair	**Stuhl**	*Stool*
Tray	**Tablett**	*Tab-let*
Wallpaper	**Tapete**	*Tap-et*
Carpet	**Teppich**	*Te-pikh*
Freezer	**Tiefkühltruhe**	*Tef-kyul-tru*
Table	**Tisch**	*Tish*
Tablecloth	**Tischtuch**	*Tish-tukh*
Toiletpaper	**Toilettenpapier**	*Toilet-n-papier*
Saucepan	**Topf**	*Topf*
Cloth	**Tuch**	*Tukh*
Door	**Tür**	*Tyur*
Curtain	**Vorhang**	*For-hang*
Washing machine	**Waschmaschine**	*Vash-mach-ine*
Wash powder	**Waschpulver**	*Vash-pol-fr*
Tap	**Wasserhahn**	*Vassr-han*
Alarm clock	**Wecker**	*Vek-r*

Getting Around

This section may prove to be the most useful for anyone travelling in any German-speaking land, as it is filled with a wide variety of very useful words and phrases that pertain to travelling.

Germany is a much frequented hotspot for travellers from all corners of the globe. Known for their austere work ethic and remarkable efficiency, the German people know how to make a nation welcoming and agreeable. One of Germany's most remarkable characteristics is how effortless the medieval intertwines with the contemporary. Stepping onto the German countryside for the first time is at once like entering an ancient fairytale, and a futuristic Asimovian wonderland. If the former, with its dense forests and pristine lakes and rivers don't sound like your ideal vacation spot, then the latter may be more your taste, with everything modernity has to offer.

There are, however, a few things the average traveller needs to know before entering Germany.

First of all, Germany is a European Union state. This means that they use the Euro as currency, among other things. Germany also happens to be a signatory of the Schengen convention. With this being said, any given national of the EU has a right to unlimited and free travel within Germany. Nationals from other western countries are, on the other hand, only entitled to 90 days of unrestricted travel with Germany. Beyond that 90 day threshold a Schengen visa is required for further stay. Nationals of most eastern countries, however, have the harshest restrictions; they have to acquire a Schengen visa to travel to Germany in the first place.

Another aspect of German culture that is very much appreciable is that it's relatively safe. With a low crime rate and virtually no natural disasters, Germany is generally much safer than lots of western nations. It is always advisable though, to err on the side of safety, to invest in travel insurance, no matter where one travels.

The intrepid traveler may or may not find it hard to nail down a time of year to visit Germany. While this is, of course, a matter of personal preference, it is generally believed that Germany is a nation that is best to be explored during the summer months.
To that end, every time of year in Germany produces its own charms. The so-called 'low' season (Nov-Mar) has the coldest weather. Ski resorts, theater, concerts, and opera are most popular during this season.

The 'mid' seasons (Apr-Jun, Sep-Oct) brings nice, mild weather and, with it, lower prices.

And finally the 'high' season (Jul and Aug) brings the best weather as well as the most energy and activity. The highest prices and the most congestion are also to be expected within this season though.

Another significant aspect to consider when travelling to this nation is, of course, the expenses involved. While Germany is not the cheapest nation to visit, there still are numerous ways to travel the land without bankrupting one's self. In fact, according to one estimate, it is possible to visit Germany for as little 40-80 US dollars a day.
Some price estimates for travelling expenses in Germany are listed below:

Accommodation:
€10-30 ($12-35) dorms
€45-65 ($50-75) budget hotels
   Mid-Range: €60-100 ($70-120)
   Splurge: €150+ ($175+)

Food (meals for one):
Street food: €2-4 ($2-5)
Cheap meal at beer hall: €9-15 ($11-18)
Restaurant: €15-20 ($18-25)
Top-rated restaurant: €100 ($115)

Transportation:
Bike Rental: €18 ($21) per day
City Transit: €1-3 ($1-4) per single ticket
Intercity Bus: €15-30 ($18-35)
Overnight buses: €20-70 ($25-82)
Trains: €40-70 ($48-82) slow
  €100+ ($120+) high-speed

As you can probably see, Germany is not only not as expensive to travel to, as the average person would guess it is, but it is, in fact, even cheaper to travel to than lots of US cities. Take New York, Boston, San Diego, and Washington D.C. for example, their average nightly rates for hotels range from $250-$370. These figures seem almost ludicrous when compared to the $70-$175 of most German cities. To add to that, the traveller is getting the added historical value of a handful of more than 1,000-year-old buildings in Germany, so to say the least, the educational and cultural value of a trip to Germany just can't be rivaled by a trip to many American cities.

When packing one's suitcase for Germany, it is important to include a wide variety of articles of clothing. The weather is rather fickle in Germany, and in every season, too; so it is best to come prepared for whatever weather mother nature has to offer.

Berlin, the capital of Germany, has a well-deserved reputation as being a great city for freelancers and otherwise creative people—with its world famous nightlife, art, museums, cafe culture, and music scene. It is also widely known for its interesting historical significance.

The demeanor of *Munich* is more staid and quieter, with the exception of its annual celebration of Oktoberfest. It holds historical buildings, museums, parks, and popular beer halls all side by side.

While Berlin and Munich are both enchanting and becoming cities, we would be remiss to not pour over some of the other great cities

Germany has to offer. These include *Hamburg*, famous for its parks, canals, and boasting the second busiest port in Europe. *Frankfurt* is a city better suited for the history and or science lover. It has a number of historical sites, science museums, and a famous restaurant scene. *Cologne* is another city well suited for the history lover. It has historical sites including its world famous cathedral. And finally, for those who want a fine mixture of modernity and nature, *Dresden* is a great city to find that balance.

One aspect of travel in Germany that is—more often than not—neglected by visitors, and also of travelers in any part of the globe, for that matter, is the natural landscapes the countryside has to offer. Germany has no shortage of natural wonders, and there are many places that a traveler can go to witness just what the country really has to offer. One spot in Germany that's perfect for those who love the outdoors is *Berchtesgaden National Park*. It is known for its dense forests, clear lakes, and huge boulders. *Lake Constance*, the largest freshwater lake in Germany, may also be a better fit for the outdoorsman.

One of the finest forests in Germany is the *Black Forest*. It is located in a mountainous region in southwest Germany, bordering France. This forest is widely known for the abundance of its megaflora and the archaic, charming villages nestled within its dense interior. This is a great spot for a slower paced vacation in a natural setting.
One cannot mention travel within Germany without a talking about the castles and palaces that inhabit the land. One of the most famous examples of these, forever memorialized by the Disney Corporation and by its architecture in and of itself, is *Neuschwanstein Castle*. This is one of the more intriguing and impressive buildings the globe has to offer and nothing can really supplement seeing it in person, so trekking to this building would be an unassailably important part of any vacation to Germany.

While the Germans, being sensible people, often speak English, (so often, in fact, that English is a mandatory subject for many of Germany's students from the fifth grade onward) the list below should still prove to be of great help for the foreigner as it includes lots of words and phrases useful in travelling.

Where?	**Wo?**	vō
I need some information.	**Ich brauche eine Auskunft**	ikh broukh-ə īnə ous'-kunft
I need help.	**Ich brauche Hilfe.**	ikh broukh-ə hilf-ə
Do you know the area?	**Kennen Sie sich hier aus?**	ken'-nen zee zikh heer ous
Am I in the right place?	**Bin ich hier richtig?**	bin ikh heer rikh'-tik
Excuse me, where is…?	**Entschuldigung, wo ist…?**	ent-shul'-dĭ-gung vō ist
Which direction is X in?	**In welcher Richtung ist X?**	in vel'-kher rĭkh'-tung ist x
Where is the [entrance/exit]?	**Wo ist der [Eingang/Ausgang]?**	vō ist dare [īn'-gong/ous'-gong]
Where is the bus stop?	**Wo ist die Bushaltestelle?**	vō ist dee boos-halt'-ə-shtell-ə
Where is the underground train (subway/metro)?	**Wo ist die U-Bahn?**	vō ist dee oo'-bon
One ticket to …, please!	**Eine Fahrkarte nach …, bitte!**	īn-ə farcart-ə bitt-ə
When does the next train for … leave?	**Wann fährt der nächste Zug nach …?**	von fairt dair näshte tzug nosh
Where does is this bus going to?	**Wohin fährt dieser Bus?**	vohin fairt deezer bus
When is this train scheduled to arrive?	**Wann kommt dieser Zug an?**	von comt deezer tzug on
I wonder where this bus goes to?	**Fährt dieser Bus nach…?**	fairt deezer bus nokh
Could I please have a map of the city?	**Darf ich bitte einen Stadtplan haben?**	darf ikh bitt-ə shtot'-plon hobb-en
Please take me to	**Bringen Sie mich**	bring-en zee

this address.	**bitte zu dieser Adresse.**	*mikh bitt-ə tzoo deez-er ad-res-sə*
I am looking for the museum/park/hotel.	**Ich suche das Museum/den Park/das Hotel.**	*ikh zookh-ə dos moo-zā-əm/dān park/dos hō-tel*
Please stop here.	**Halten Sie bitte hier an.**	*holt-en zee bitt-ə heer on*
To the city center, please.	**Zum Stadtzentrum, bitte.**	*tzoom shtat-tzen'-troom bit-tə*
To the train station, please.	**Zum Bahnhof, bitte.**	*tzoom bon-hof bit-tə*
To the airport, please.	**Zum Flughafen, bitte.**	*tzoom floog'-hof-en*
Where is a good bakery?	**Wo ist eine leckere Bäckerei?**	*vō ist ī-nə lěk'-er-ə běk'-er-ī*
Where is a close gas station?	**Wo ist die nächste Tankstelle?**	*vō ist der nākh'-stə tonk'-shtell-ə*
At what place is the bank?	**Wo ist die Bank?**	*vō ist dee bahnk*
Is the airport far away?	**Ist der Flughafen weit weg?**	*ist der floog'-haf-fen vīt vek*
I would like to be shown?	**Können Sie mir das zeigen?**	*cunn-en zee meer doss tzī'-gən*
Do I have to change?	**Muss ich umsteigen?**	*moos ikh um-shtī'-gən*
It's there. / There it is.	**Es ist da. / Da ist es.**	*ess ist dah/dah ist ess*
around the corner	**um die Ecke**	*um dee ě-kə*
to the left	**nach links**	*nokh linx*
to the right	**nach rechts**	*nakh rekhs*
straight ahead	**geradaus**	*ger-ah'-dous*
upstairs	**oben**	*ō'-ben*
downstairs	**unten**	*un'-ten*
back	**zurück**	*tzoo-rook'*
north	**Nord**	*nord*
south	**Süd**	*zoot*

east	**Ost**	*ōst*
West	**West**	*vest*
Brochure	**Broschüre**	*Broschüre*
Campsite	**Campingplatz**	*Campingplatz*
Reception(ist)	**Empfang(sdame)**	*Empfang(sdame)*
Holiday	**Ferien**	*Ferien*
Lost Property Office	**Fundbüro**	*Fundbüro*
Guest	**Gast**	*Gast*
Host	**Gastgeber**	*Gastgeber*
Restaurant/ Pub	**Gaststätte**	*Gaststätte*
Luggage	**Gepäck**	*Gepäck*
Map	**Landkarte**	*Landkarte*
Place	**Ort**	*Ort*
Passport	**Pass (reisepass)**	*Pass (reisepass)*
Identity Card	**Personalausweis**	*Personalausweis*
Traveller	**Reisende(r)**	*Reisende(r)*
Destination	**Reiseziel**	*Reiseziel*
Cheque Book	**Scheckheft**	*Scheckheft*
Sleeping Bag	**Schlafsack**	*Schlafsack*
To stay the night	**übernatchten**	*übernatchten*
Accomodation	**Unterkunft**	*Unterkunft*
Maid	**Zimmermädchen**	*Zimmermädchen*
Overcast	**Bedeckt**	*Bee-dekt*
To thunder	**Donnern**	*Don-uhrn*
Dark	**Dunkel**	*Dun-kel*
To freeze	**Frieren**	*Fri-rn*
Thunderstorm	**Gewitter**	*Ge-wit-r*
Hail	**Hagel**	*Hagl*
Hot	**Heiß**	*Hass*
Heat	**Hitze**	*Hit-z*
Cold	**Kalte**	*Kahlt*
Climate	**Klima**	*Klim-ah*
Cool	**Kühl**	*Kyuhl*
Wet	**Nass**	*Nass*
Fog(gy)/ Mist(y)	**Nebel (nebelig)**	*Ne-bel (ne-bel-*

		ig)
Rain(coat)	**Regen (mantel)**	*Re-gen (mant-l)*
Umbrella	**Regenschirm**	*Re-gen-shirm*
To rain	**Regnen**	*Reg-nen*
To shine	**Scheinen**	*Shan-en*
Snow	**Schnee**	*Shn-ee*
To snow	**Schneien**	*Shn<u>e</u>n*
Sun	**Sonne**	*S<u>o</u>n*
Sunny	**Sonnig**	*S<u>o</u>n-ig*
Stormy	**Sturm/ Stürmisch**	*Sturm/ Styur-mish*
Weather (forecast)	**Wetter (bericht/ vorhersage)**	*Vet-r (b-rikh/ vor-hr-sage)*
Cloud (less)	**Wolke (wolkenlos)**	*Vohlk (Vohlk-n-los)*

Lodging & Hotels

This one relates to the previous section in its utility for travellers. The words and phrases listed below are useful to anyone lodging in any German-speaking areas.

Are there any available rooms?	**Sind noch Zimmer frei?**	*zint noch tzimmer frī*
What does a double room cost?	**Wie viel kostet ein Doppelzimmer?**	*vee feel cost'-et īn dop'-pel-tzim-mer*
What does a single room cost?	**Wie viel kostet ein Einzelzimmer?**	*vee feel costet īn īn'-tzel-tzim-mer*
When is breakfast?	**Wann gibt es Frühstück?**	*von gibt ess froo'-shtook/ah-bent-es-sen*
Does this room come with ...? (Has this room...)	**Hat das Zimmer ...?**	*Hot dos tzim'-mer*
balcony	**einen Balkon**	*īn-en bol-cone'*
television	**einen Fernseher**	*īn-en fairn'-zā-er*
WiFi	**Wifi**	*vī-fi*

air conditioning	**eine Klimaanlage**	*īn-ə clee'-mon-lag-ə*
I'm staying for ... night.	**Ich bleibe für ... Nacht.**	*ikh blīb'-ə fyur... nakht*
one night	**eine Nacht**	*īn'-ə nokht*
three nights	**drei Nächte**	*drī někht'-ə*
I would like a room.	**Ich hätte gern ein Zimmer.**	*ikh hět-tə gairn īn tzim-mer*
I will stay for [one night/two nights/three nights].	**Ich bleibe [eine Nacht/zwei Nächte/drei Nächte].**	*ikh blīb [īn-ə nokht/tzwī někht-ə/drī někht-ə*
Is breakfast included?	**Ist Frühstück inklusiv?**	*ist froo'-shtook in'-kloos-eef*
Would you please wake me up at 8 o'clock?	**Können Sie mich um acht Uhr wecken?**	*Kun-nen zee mikh um x oor věk'-en*
room service	**Zimmerdienst**	*tzim'-mer-deenst*
shower	**Dusche**	*doosh*
single room	**Einzelzimmer**	*īn'-tzel-tzim-mer*
air conditioning	**Klimaanlage**	*kleem-a-ahn'-lag-ə*
key	**Schlüssel**	*shloo'-sel*

Eating Out

There are lots of mannerisms that differentiate German dining from dining in other countries. Featured below is a short list of these mannerisms useful for anyone not familiar with the German dining experience:

Upon entering a restaurant in German-speaking Europe, it is not advisable to wait to be seated. It is generally expected of diners to find tables on their own. Servers seldom suggest tables to incoming diners because they are usually busy with current diners. Unless the diner sees the words spelled out: 'please wait to be seated,' he or she should find his or her own seat.

Most Americans have come to expect a glass of water with every meal that they eat out. Most Europeans, on the other hand, avoid drinking tap water with any of their meals, not out of concern for safety or hygiene, but because they don't like the idea of having such a bland liquid with their food. They prefer to diversify with their drinks.
If water is requested, it is only rarely tap water, but usually *mineralwasser* (or mineral water) instead. Americans requesting tap water at public eateries in Europe are usually met with looks of disgust. Mineral water is the preferred drink.

Germans are known for having a very practical and also very amiable custom of sitting with the strangers around them while eating at their beer gardens and restaurants, where long tables and numerous empty seats are common.
Bread rolls are other extras that are usually not free in Germany, or most of Europe for that matter. While they are supposedly free in America, they are often still included in the price of the full meal, so the only difference in this European custom is its relative honesty and straightforwardness.

À la carte dining is the most common type of purchase in German-speaking Europe. Usually, any given side dishes are ordered and paid for independently of the main course that the diner chooses. In short, a diner pays only for what he or she consumes in Germany, which can be either very beneficial or detrimental to him or her.

That, in turn, brings us now to the all-important topic of payment in German dining.
As is common in America, the payments and tipping for meals in German-speaking Europe are both done at the table eaten at, and the server commonly carries a money pouch holstered around his or her waist as the work is done. However, unlike in America, the checks always have to be requested after a meal. Servers don't bring them about until they are.

The average and righteous tipping amount in Germany is +-15%, as is the case in America, but tips are and should never be left on the table. As is the case in America, it is not required that any given diner tips his or her server, but it is also generally frowned upon when a diner is remiss to reward a server's good work. Another fact that also shares similitude with American dining is the fact that servers in Germany live meagerly off of mostly tips, and that it is very important that they are rewarded for their work.

When paying with a credit card in Germany, the tipping process is slightly different than it is in America. The diner typically is required to tell the server the amount of the tip before the card is swiped. It is, of course, always ideal to pay the tip in cash, as the server doesn't have to pay income taxes on cash tips.

As was mentioned before, sales tax is included in the price of nearly everything purchased in Germany before the transaction. This sales tax is fairly high, however, at 19%.

Another point that has been mentioned is the fact that many German stores do not accept credit cards. Unfortunately for most Americans who live and die by electronic currencies, the same is true for many German restaurants of all tiers. This is why it is wise to ask about electronic payments before ordering.

Now that we know some important points on dining in Germany, it may also be helpful to go over some of what the German cuisine includes.

Next to some of its European neighbors (such as Italy, or France, or Spain just to name a few) Germany's cuisine may seem boring or even unappetizing to many foreigners, but nothing could be further from the truth. Their food has, however, built up quite a well-deserved reputation for its hardiness and the relative simplicity of its recipes. But, for whatever one's palate desires, there is sure to be a German dish willing and ready to meet any given needs.

The first food to be mentioned is a very famous one in the US, and all throughout the world for that matter. It is the *bratwürst*. This is a remarkably popular German sausage, the best of which supposedly come from Nürnberg. These are usually made from pork shoulder, veal shoulder, pork fat, and spices.

Another very popular German dish goes by the name of *spätzle*. This is a vegetarian (rare in German cuisine) pasta dish consisting of eggs, flour, salt, and water. Like any pasta, it is best served as a side or a compliment to another dish. It is also good when served with cheese alone. Again, the beauty of some of Germany's greatest food lies within their simplicity.

But any discussion surrounding German pastas cannot be complete without the mention of *maultaschen*. This is a great ravioli dish which can be compared to a hot pocket. It can be, and usually is, stuffed with minced meat, sauerkraut, spinach, or really any other food for that matter. They can also be boiled or fried, and served as a main dish or as a side dish. They are great no matter how the diner takes them.

And lastly, also perhaps most famously, we come to the *bretzel*, or pretzel in English. One feature of the German *bretzel* that distinguishes it from its American cousin is its robustness. This is a classic snack food that can be found at fairs, carnivals, sporting events, virtually any public happening across the globe, and for good reason.
And now that we have been over German dining and some of the nation's foods, we can
at last come to some vocabulary over German dining:

Are you hungry? (informal)	**Hast du Hunger?**	*host doo hun-ger*
Are you hungry? (formal)	**Haben Sie Hunger?**	*hob'-ben zee hun-ger*
Are you thirsty? (informal)	**Hast du Durst?**	*host doo durst*

Are you thirsty? (formal)	**Haben Sie Durst?**	*hob'-ben zee durst*
Shall we get something to eat/drink together?	**Wollen wir etwas zusammen essen/trinken gehen?**	*vol-len veer et-vos tzoo-sam'-men es-sen/trink-en gā-en*
Breakfast	**Frühstück**	*froo'-shtook*
Lunch	**Mittagessen**	*mitt'-ak-es-sen*
Dinner	**Abendessen**	*ah'-bent-es-sen*
A table for one/two/three..., please.	**Einen Tisch für eine Person/zwei/drei ..., bitte.**	*ī' nen tish fyur īn-ĕ pair-zōn/tzvī/drī... bitt'-ə*
A menu, please.	**Die Speisekarte, bitte.**	*dee shpī'-zə-cart-ə, bitt-ə*
Waiter! / Waitress!	**Kellner!/Kellnerin!**	*kell'-ner/kell'-ner-in*
I'd like....	**Ich hätte gern....**	*ikh hêt-ə gern*
I'd like....	**Ich möchte gern....**	*ikh mukht-ə gern*
Nothing for me, thank you.	**Für mich nichts, danke.**	*fyur mikh nikhts donk-ə*
Would you recommend something?	**Könnten Sie etwas empfehlen?**	*kun-ten zee êt-vas êmp-fā'-len*
I only eat vegetables.	**Ich bin Vegetarier.**	*ikh bin vā'-gə-tair-ier*

Do you have food for vegetarians?	**Haben Sie vegetarisches Essen?**	*hobben zee vā-gə-tair'-ish-ess ess-en*
Is that gluten-free?	**Ist das glutenfrei?**	*ist dos gloot'-en-frī*
I am allergic to X.	**Ich bin allergisch gegen X.**	*ikh bin all-er-gish gā-gen X*
Nuts	**Nusse**	*noo-sə*
Shellfish	**Schalentiere**	*shol-en-teer'-ə*
Dairy	**Milch**	*Milkh*
Strawberries	**Erdbeeren**	*aird-beer'-en*
Gluten	**Gluten**	*gloot'-en*
Okay, I will take that.	**Gut, das nehme ich.**	*goot, dos nā-mə ikh*
I'd like to have some X please.	**Ich hätte gerne X.**	*ikh hĕt-tə gern-ə X*
Chicken	**Hühnchen**	*hoon'-shyen*
Pork	**Schweinefleisch**	*shvīn'-ə-flīsh*
Beef	**Rindfleisch**	*rĭnd'-flīsh*
Soup	**Suppe**	*zoop'-ə*
Pasta	**Nudeln**	*nood'-eln*
Vegetables	**Gemüse**	*ge-myooz'-ə*
Spicy	**scharf**	*sharf*

Sweet	**süß**	*soos*
Sour	**sauer**	*sou'-er*
Salt	**Salz**	*Zoltz*
Pepper	**Pfeffer**	*feff'-ər*
Sugar	**Zucker**	*tzoo'-kər*
Napkin	**Serviette**	*ser-vee-et'*
Plate	**Teller**	*tell'-er*
Fork	**Gabel**	*go'-bel*
Spoon	**Löffel**	*luff'-əl*
knife	**Messer**	*mess'-ər*
Glass	**Glas**	*glos*
Cup	**Tasse**	*toss'-ə*
Beer	**Bier**	*beer*
Wine	**Wein**	*vīn*
tap water	**Leitungswasser**	*lī'-tungs-voss-er*
A glass of water, please.	**Ein Glas Wasser, bitte.**	*īn glos voss'-ər bitt-ə*
[Sparkling/not sparkling], please.	**[Mit/ohne] Sprudel, bitte.**	*[mit/ōn-ə] shproo'-dl bit-tə*
A beer please!	**Ein Bier bitte!**	*īn beer bit-tə*

What's on tap?	"Was gibt's vom Fass?"	vos gibts vom fos
With lactose-free milk, please.	Mit laktosefreier Milch, bitte.	mit lak'-tōs-frī-ər milkh bitt-ə
Another one, please!	Noch eine, bitte!	nokh īn'-ə bit-ə
Another of the same, please.	Das Gleiche nochmal bitte.	dos glīkh nokh-mol bit-tə
Can I get that without tomato?	Kriege ich das auch ohne Tomaten?	kreeg-ə ikh dos oukh ō-nə tō-mot-ten
Do you have dessert too?	Gibt's auch Nachtisch?	gibts oukh nokh-tish
Can you wrap that up to go?	Können Sie das einpacken?	kun-nen zee dos īn'-pok-en
That was delicious!	Das hat hervorragend geschmeckt!	dos hot hair-for'-ra-gent ge-shmekt
One coffee, please!	Einen Kaffee bitte!	īn-en kof-fā bit-tə
Excuse me please.	Entschuldigen Sie bitte.	ênt-shool'-də-gen zee bit-tə
Could you show me to the restroom?	Wo ist die Toilette?	vō isst dee toy-lett'-ə
men	Herren/Männer	hair'-en/měn'-ər

women	**Damen/Frauen**	*dah'-men/frou'-en*
I am full.	**Ich bin satt.**	*ikh bin zot*
Please bring the check.	**Die Rechnung bitte.**	*dē rêkh-nung bitt-ə*
A receipt, please.	**Eine Quittung bitte.**	*īn-ə kvĭ'-tung bitt-ə*
Could I get a receipt, please?	**Darf ich eine Quittung haben, bitte?**	*darf ikh īn-ə kvĭ'-tung bitt-ə*
Enjoy. (Good appetite)	**Guten Appetit.**	*goo-ten âp-ə-tēt'*
Cheers!	**Zum Wohl!**	*tzoom vōl*
Cheers!	**Prost!**	*Prōst*
Flame	**Flamme**	*Flamme*
Bottle	**Flasche**	*Flash*
Fresh	**Frisch**	*Frish*
Dish/ Course	**Gericht**	*Jeri-kt*
Jar/ Pot	**Glas**	*Glass*
To grill/ Barbeque	**Grillen**	*Grill-an*
Snack (bar)	**Imbiss (stube)**	*Em-biss (stoob)*
Canteen	**Kantine**	*Kan-teen*
Kitchen	**Küche**	*Koo-ch*

Delicious	**Lecker**	*Le-kerr*
Spoon	**Löffel**	*Law-fell*
Meal	**Mahlzeit**	*Mall-zat*
Knife	**Messer**	*Mes-ser*
Dessert	**Nachtisch**	*Nak-tish*
To taste	**Schmecken**	*Shmek-in*
Fast-food Restaurant	**Schnellimbiss**	*Shnel-lim-biss*
Bowl	**Schüssel**	*Shoo-sell*
Self-service	**Selbstbedienung**	*Selbst-bedie-nung*
Menu	**Speisekarte**	*Space-kart*
Supermarket	**Supermarkt**	*Super-market*

Emergencies

This section is one of great utility not only for German language learners, but also for anyone who may have friends or relatives who speak only German. It is a list of words and phrases useful in emergency or crisis situations.

help	**hilfe**	*hilf-ə*
fire	**feuer**	*foy'-er*
(informal) Call the police!	**Ruf die Polizei!**	*roof dee po-leet-zī'*
Stop! A thief!	**Halt! Ein Dieb!**	*halt īn deeb*
I am getting sick.	**Ich bin krank.**	*ikh bin kronk*
I don't feel too well.	**Mir geht es nicht so gut.**	*meer gāt es nikht zō goot*
She has gotten	**Sie ist krank**	*zee ist kronk ge-vor'-*

sick.	**geworden.**	*den*
He needs a doctor.	**Er braucht einen Arzt.**	*air broucht īn'-en artst*
Where's the closest hospital?	**Wo ist das nächste Krankenhaus?**	*vō ist doss nāshte cron'-ken-hous*
My wallet has been lost.	**Ich habe mein Portemonnaie verloren.**	*ikh hobb-ə mīn port-e-mon-ī'] fair-lor'-en*
Someone took my bag.	**Jemand hat meine Tasche genommen.**	*yā'-mont hot mīn-ə tosh'-ə ge-nō'-men*
Where is the hospital?	**Wo ist das Krankenhaus?**	*vō ist dos kronk'-en-hous*
Where is the pharmacy?	**Wo ist die Apotheke?**	*vō ist dē ah-pō-tāk'*
Do you have aspirin?	**Haben Sie Aspirin?**	*hobb-en zee asp-ir-in*
This is an emergency.	**Es ist ein Notfall.**	*ess ist īn nōt'-fol*
I am lost.	**Ich habe mich verlaufen.**	*ikh hob-ə mikh fer-louf'-en*

Holiday Greetings

Public holidays in Germany, along with their celebrations, differ from state to state. While the most common christian holidays of the western world are celebrated eagerly in each and every state in Germany, there is still variance in the celebration of more minor holidays from state to state.

Major holidays which are celebrated in every state in Germany (Baden-Wüttemberg, Bavaria, Berlin, Brandenburg, Bremen, Hamburg, Hesse, Mecklenburg-Vorpommern, Lower Saxony, North Rhine-Westphalia, Rhineland-Palatinate, Saarland, Saxony, Saxony-Anhalt, Schleswig-Holstein, and Free State of Thuringia) are listed below:

- *New Year's Day* (Neujahrstag)
- *Good Friday* (Karfreitag)
- *Easter Monday* (Ostermontag)
- *Labour Day* (Tag Der Arbeit)
- *Ascension Day* (Christi Himmelfahrt)
- *White Monday* (Pfingstmontag)
- *German Unity Day* (Tag Der Deutschen Einheit)
- *Christmas Day* (Weihnachtstag)
- *St. Stephen's Day/ Boxing Day* (Zweiter Weihnachtsfeiertag)

More minor holidays which are not necessarily and officially celebrated in every state, but are still important days of the German year are listed below:

- *Epiphany* (Heilige Drei Könige)
- *Corpus Christi* (Fronleichnam)
- *Peace Festival* (Friedensfest)
- *Assumption Day* (Mariä Himmelfahrt)
- *Reformation Day* (Reformationstag)
- *All Saints Day* (Allerheiligen)
- *Repentance and Prayer Day* (Buß- und Bettag)

Of all the holidays previously mentioned, a small number of them are known as *stille tage* (or quiet days). On these days, louder public functions, such as public dancing events, public concerts, music at inns, etc., are prohibited by law.

These holidays are as follows:

Good Friday, Repentance and Prayer Day, All Saints Day, Memorial Day, Totensonntag, Christmas Eve, Ash Wednesday, Holy Thursday, Holy Saturday, All Souls Day.
Another category of holiday in Germany is that of the Flag Days (or Beflaggung Stage).

While the highest of governmental facilities are required to show their flags on every day of each year, on the days listed below, flag showing is required by federal decree for everyone:

Holocaust Memorial Day, Labor Day, Europe Day, Constitution Day, Remembrance of June 17th, World Refugee Day, Remembrance of July 20th, German Unity Day, Memorial Day (half-mast), and Election Day.

In addition to the official public holidays previously mentioned, there are a small number of unofficial German holidays that are worthy of note.

These are as follows:

Carnival Monday (or Mardis Gras as it is known throughout many parts of the US and other parts of the globe) traditionally starts on 11/11 at 11.11 am.

Presently, Christmas Eve has been becoming more of its own holiday than not, as it is more and more uncommon to work on that day and schools are always closed.

This is another section that is useful not only for German language learners, but anyone who knows German speakers and wants to wish them happy holidays.

Happy birthday!	**Herzlichen Glückwunsch zum Geburtstag!**	*hairtz'-lich-en glook'-vunsh tzoom ge-boorts-tok*
Merry Christmas!	**Frohe Weihnachten!**	*frō'-ə vī'-nach-ten*
Happy New Year!	**Frohes Neues!**	*frō'-ə noy'-ess*
Happy Easter!	**Frohe Ostern!**	*frō'-ə ō'-stern*
Congratulations!	**Herzliche Glückwünsche!**	*hairtz'-likh-ə glook'-voonsh-ə*
New Year's Day	**Neujahrstag**	*Noo-jahr-staag*
Good Friday	**Karfreitag**	*Kaar-fra-tag*
Easter Monday	**Ostermontag**	*Oostr-mon-tag*
Labor Day	**Tag Der Arbeit**	*Tag-dr-rbat*
Ascension Day	**Christi Himmelfahrt**	*Kristi Himel-fart*
White Monday	**Pfingstmontag**	*fingst-mon-tag*
German Unity Day	**Tag Der Deutschen Einheit**	*Tag dr dooych-n in-hat*
Christmas Day	**Weihnachtstag**	*Vah-nacht-stag*
St. Stephen's Day/ Boxing Day	**Zweiter Weihnachtsfeiertag**	*sva-tr vah-nachts-faer-tag*
Epiphany	**Heilige Drei Könige**	*Ha-lig dri kyon-ig*
Corpus Christi	**Fronleichnam**	*Fron-lach-nam*
Peace Festival	**Friedensfest**	*Frad-ns-fest*
Assumption Day	**Mariä Himmelfahrt**	*Maria himl-fart*
Reformation Day	**Reformationstag**	*Re-form-ation-stag*
All Saints Day	**Allerheiligen**	*Alr-hali-gen*
Repentance and Prayer Day	**Buß- und Bettag**	*Bus und beet-ag*

Chapter 8: Putting it All Together

Basic Conversations

An informal introduction might go something like this:
- **Das ist mein Freund(m)/meine Freundin(f)...**
  (dos ist mī-ne friyn-den/mīn froint)
  (This is my friend...)
- **Hallo, es freut mich dich kennenzulernen.**
  (Hallo, es froit mikh dikh kennenzulairnen)
  (Hello, it's nice to meet you.)
  OR
- **Freut mich.**
  (froit mikh)
  (Pleased to meet you.)
- **Mich auch.**
  (mikh oukh)
  (Me too.)

If the situation calls for a more formal introduction, you might say (or hear) this:
- **Guten Abend! Darf ich Ihnen... vorstellen?**
  (goot-en o-bent darf ikh ee-nen... for-shtel-en)
  (May I introduce you...?)
- **Freut mich Sie kennenzulernen.**
  (froit mikh zee ken'-nen-tzu-lern-nen)
  (Pleased to make your acquaintance.)
- **Meinerseits./Ganz meinerseits.**
  (mī-ner-zīts)/(gǎntz mī-ner-zīts)
  (Me too.)

"Likewise" is not the actual translation of the German word **"meinerseits."** **Meinerseits** literally means "mine." **Ganz meinerseits** literally means "all mine," as in, "the pleasure is all mine."

The conversation might continue in a similar vein:

- **Ist der Platz noch frei?**
  (ist der plots nokh frī)
  (Is this seat still free?)
- **Ja, bitte.**
  (yah, <u>bit</u>-tə)
  (Yes, please.)

"Please" is used slightly more loosely in German than in English. You might think of it as "Please feel free" in this case.

This conversation would be very different among younger people at a party or some other informal setting.
- **Wie heißt du?**
  (vee hīst doo)
  (What's your name?)
- **Ich heiße _____. Und du?**
  (ikh hīs-sə _____. unt doo)
  (I am called _____. And you?)
- **_____. Wer ist das?**
  (ver ist dos)
  (_____. Who is that?)
- **Das ist meine Freundin _____.**
  (dos ist <u>mī</u>-nə <u>froin</u>-din)
  (This is my friend _____.)

Chapter 9: Continuing to Learn

The German language is a beautiful and elegant tongue. Learning a new language is never easy, but if you have the desire (or possibly the necessity) to continue this undertaking, here are some tips to help you along.

The more immersed you are in the language, the faster and easier you will learn. If you are living (even for a short time) in a German-speaking environment, you will have a leg up, but it takes a bit of discipline. As frustrating as it can be at times, try to only watch television and listen to the radio in German.

Concentrate at first on distinguishing sounds, then words. This is easier said than done! Even though the letters (or most of them, anyway) are the same as in English, they often somehow manage to sound different coming out of "foreign" mouths. Sounds are made in slightly different positions in the mouth, which, while they're basically the same sounds, they're not quite as easy to recognize. This will make it sound like the other person is speaking very quickly, but the truth is that you are simply listening slowly, due to the fact that you're having to match the sounds they're making with the sounds you're expecting, and when they don't match exactly it causes you to have to work harder.

Don't feel bad if you can't understand every word, or even if you miss words that you think you should have caught. When you're learning a language, you are listening to every sound, trying to separate out each word, and translate it. When you are fluent, you don't need to do that. You can "guess" at a word by only hearing a portion of it, so it isn't necessary to hear the whole word to understand it.

So since your listening skills are being strained, it's counterproductive (and extremely frustrating!) to try to catch every word. Instead, focus on picking out a word here and there. It doesn't matter if you can't follow every conversation. Learning to recognize individual words is a good way to speed up your listening skills and you'll find that it won't be too long before you graduate to being able to understand whole sentences.

If you don't live in a German-speaking place where it will be always in the background, you can still immerse yourself to a small degree. Find German videos online, German music or eBooks. It is much easier today than it ever has been before to find resources for spoken German, and the more you listen, even if you're not consciously learning, the faster you'll be able to pick it up in the long run.

Another way to improve your skills, specifically in vocabulary and sentence building, is to copy (preferably by physically writing them out) German stories or news articles (or lessons). Writing German sentences will give you a feel for the flow while teaching you word endings and vocabulary. Don't forget to stop and read the sentences out loud so you can practice your pronunciation at the same time! It's also important to get in the habit of analyzing sentences as you're reading or copying them. You don't want to do it necessarily with everything you read (or you'll quickly lose your desire to continue), but make sure you set aside some time to go through each word and select sentences to quiz yourself on what endings there are, what cases the words are in, why the word order is the way it is, etc. The more analytical you can be, the more it will make sense to you and the less "unnatural" it will feel to speak.

It probably won't feel like it's going as quickly as you'd like. Languages are incredibly complicated things with thousands of words to memorize, not to mention wrapping your mind around pronoun endings, tenses, and which prepositions go with which case. When speaking, if you're unsure of a word or a conjugation, it's better to toss in the English word than to halt the conversation while you look it up. Your listeners will probably either understand or be able to guess what you meant, and will most likely either provide the word for you or simply ignore the switch. The important thing is to be able to make yourself understood, not to be perfect. You forgive non-native English speakers when they make a mistake, so allow yourself some lapses as well. They are more likely to respect your commitment to learning than to deride your blunders.

You may feel like you're wasting your time and you'll never get there, but take heart. After all, if small children can learn German, surely you can too!

German Short Stories

8 Easy to Follow Stories with English Translation for Effective German Learning Experience

© Copyright 2018 by Dave Smith — All rights reserved.

The following eBook is reproduced below with the goal of providing information that is as accurate and reliable as possible. Regardless, purchasing this eBook can be seen as consent to the fact that both the publisher and the author of this book are in no way experts on the topics discussed within and that any recommendations or suggestions that are made herein are for entertainment purposes only. Professionals should be consulted as needed prior to undertaking any of the action endorsed herein.

This declaration is deemed fair and valid by both the American Bar Association and the Committee of Publishers Association and is legally binding throughout the United States.

Furthermore, the transmission, duplication or reproduction of any of the following work including specific information will be considered an illegal act irrespective of if it is done electronically or in print. This extends to creating a secondary or tertiary copy of the work or a recorded copy and is only allowed with an expressed written consent from the Publisher. All additional rights reserved.

The information in the following pages is broadly considered to be truthful and accurate account of facts, and as such any inattention, use or misuse of the information in question by the reader will render any resulting actions solely under their purview. There are no scenarios in which the publisher or the original author of this work can be in any fashion deemed liable for any hardship or damages that may befall them after undertaking information described herein.

Additionally, the information in the following pages is intended only for informational purposes and should thus be thought of as universal. As befitting its nature, it is presented without assurance regarding its prolonged validity or interim quality. Trademarks that are mentioned are done without written consent and can in no way be considered an endorsement from the trademark holder.

Introduction

Congratulations on downloading *German Short Stories* , and thank you for doing so. The German language is a very fascinating language that is at once incredibly useful and feasible for most native English speakers to learn. In downloading this book, the reader can gain an advantage in their communication skills and can also benefit from the innumerable neurobiological advantages which come with learning a second language. The stories featured in this book are at once very entertaining and extremely meaningful, while the tips and grammatical notes featured in each chapter are a potentially irreplaceable asset to any ambitious reader trying to learn the German language.

The following chapters will feature eight selected short stories, presented first in their original German texts followed by their English translations. Finally, each chapter closes off with some grammatical and critical notes on the texts. The purpose of the first two parts is to provide comparative texts for the reader who is attempting to learn German. The last section provides the reader with educational resources for deciphering all the technical details of the texts. It also offers brief plot outlines.

The mention of the German short story genre may harken the educated reader back to the stereotypically doldrum nature of *The Grimm's Fairy Tales* or other similar collections, but none of such stories have been included in this book. The tales featured here are written on a more contemporary note, making them more useful and relevant to the modern reader and learner. It may be noted that the objective of this book is to provide the most relevant information possible to the casual and modern learner. In this book, you will find none of the esoteric verbiages meant for the professional linguist's consumption.

To that end, this book will provide information useful for the beginner or intermediate learner. It is also an entertaining depository of some of the better literature that the German people have to offer; a big task, but one which has been undertaken regardless. As was mentioned before, this book includes eight German short stories. Their titles are as follows: "Daisy Macbeth" by Crystal Jones, "Die Andernacher Bäckersjungen" by H.A. Guerber, "Einkaufen im Supermarkt" (Anonymous), "Unser Haus" (Anonymous), "Die Suche Nach Lorna" by Crystal Jones, "Der Hausvater" by H.A. Guerber, "Das Reiterbild in Düsseldorf" by H.A. Guerber, and "Der Pfannkuchen" by H.A. Guerber.

Chapter One: Daisy Macbeth

German text:

Daisy schaute die Kleider im Schaufenster von Bronzettis Lieblingseis mit drei Geschmacksrichtungen. Sie ging nie in den Laden, ihre Preise waren zu hoch für sie.

"Ich muss zugeben, dass italienische Stile sehr nett sind, aber man muss ziemlich schlank sein, um in sie hineinzukommen," Daisy murmelte vor sich hin. Es war nicht so, dass Daisy fett war, sie war durchschnittlich groß, aber sicherlich nicht hauchdünn, wie die meisten Modelle. Sie sagte zu sich selbst: "Mm, dieser Zweiteiler ist ein schöner Schatten."

Hinter ihrem Rücken hört sie: "Kay, ich habe nicht erwartet, dich hier zu sehen—oh, sorry, du bist nicht Kay, oder?"

Daisy drehte sich um, um zu sehen, wer mit ihr sprach. Es war ein ziemlich schäbig aussehen der, bärtiger Mann im Alter von etwa fünfzig Jahren. Er war eindeutig afrikanischen Ursprungs und hatte einen starken südlichen Akzent. Trotz seiner Kleidung trug er eine Brille einer berühmten italienischen Marke, von der Daisy wusste, dass sie extrem teuer war.

"Nein, in der Tat."

Daisy war es nicht gewohnt, mitten auf der High Street geplaudert zu werden und in Richtung ihrer Lieblingseisdiele zu laufen.

"Bitte entschuldigen Sie, Miss... äh, ich bin Filmregisseurin und..."

"Nein, danke, ich bin nicht interessiert. Auf Wiedersehen."

"Nein, du verstehst nicht. Das bin ich wirklich. Ich bin Lawrence

Baker," sagte der Mann Daisy in der Hoffnung, dass die Erwähnung seines Namens sein seltsames Verhalten erklären würde.

"Und ich bin Privatdetektiv!" erwiderte Daisy.

"Oh, das spielt keine Rolle, du wirst genau das Gleiche tun," antwortete Lawrence.

Daisy war ziemlich gut darin, lästige Leute loszuwerden, aber dieses Mal war sie ein wenig neugierig, was hinter dieser Art von Beharrlichkeit steckt.

"Nennen Sie mich Lawrence," fügte der Mann hinzu. "Falls du noch nie von mir gehört hast, ich habe eine Besetzung von *The Tempest* in Harlem inszeniert."

Daisy liebte es, Shakespeare auf der Leinwand zu sehen und hatte den Film tatsächlich gesehen.

"Ich mochte deinen Film sehr, aber ich bin nicht Kay und... oh, du hast nicht von Kay Bartok gesprochen, der kanadischen Schauspielerin in Macbeth, oder? Das hast du auch gemacht, oder?"

"Ja," Lawrence Baker lächelte. Daisy hatte seinen Tag gemacht. "Ich fürchte, meine Filme machen nicht viel Geld, aber es macht mir Freude, eine Engländerin sagen zu hören, dass ihr mindestens einer davon gefallen hat. Aber zurück zum Geschäft. Ich hielt Sie für Kay. Und ich hatte eine wunderbare Idee. Möchtest du für den Rest der Woche ihr Double sein?" Daisy war fassungslos. Mr. Lawrence fuhr fort: "Dein Gesicht ist nicht genau wie ihres, aber du hast einen identischen Körperbau und nur die gleichen langen hellbraunen Haare. Weißt du, Kay, ist etwas heruntergekommen und sie braucht dringend eine Pause. Die Sache ist die, dass sie in den nächsten Tagen viele Engagements hat, denn wir sind hier, um unseren neuesten Film *Back to the Jungle with a Modem* zu promoten."

"Nun, ich agiere wirklich nicht als Beruf—zumindest manchmal, wenn ich einen Fall untersuche, aber..." sagte Daisy.

"Schau, warum trinken wir nicht eine Tasse Kaffee da drüben," wies Lawrence auf ein Café auf der anderen Straßenseite hin. "Kay trifft mich in diesem Laden, weil sie zuerst einkaufen gehen wollte. Schau, da ist sie, geht jetzt in den Coffee-Shop."

Lawrence war der gesprächige Typ, der nie ein Nein als Antwort akzeptieren würde, und Daisy war ziemlich fasziniert von der ganzen Sache, ihr war nie eine solche Gelegenheit geboten worden, also beschloss sie, Kay Bartok zu treffen. Als sie der Schauspielerin vorgestellt wurde, sah Daisy, dass ihre Gesichtszüge anders waren und dass Kay Bartok mindestens fünfzehn Jahre älter war, aber körperlich waren sie sich tatsächlich sehr ähnlich. Kay Bartok hatte einen starken kanadischen Akzent.

"Sie sind also ein Privatdetektiv, Miss Hamilton. Wie interessant. Du musst dich von Zeit zu Zeit in sehr gefährliche Situationen bringen."

Daisy fand Gefallen an dieser liebenswürdigen Dame, die die Menschen ansah, als ob sie sich aufrichtig für das interessierte, was sie sagten.

"Kay, was meinst du, Miss Hamilton könnte ein schweres Augen-Make-up auftragen, einen Gesichtsschutz-Hut tragen und genau wie du aussehen."

"Einen Moment, Mr. Baker, ich arbeite als Privatdetektiv und nicht als Film-Doppelgänger..."

"Schau, Daisy, wir könnten dich bezahlen, als ob du etwas untersuchen würdest. Du würdest uns einen großen Gefallen tun," Lawrence bestand darauf.

Daisy zögerte: Sie hatte in diesem Moment nur einen Fall zur Hand und so konnte sie einige Büromöbel bezahlen, die sie lange Zeit sehr dringend gebraucht hatte. Berge von Akten waren überall, und ihr

Faxgerät funktionierte nicht.

"Nun"—antwortete sie—"Ich wollte gerade in Urlaub fahren, aber ich konnte es für ein paar Tage verschieben."

Lawrence Baker lächelte triumphierend: "Kay, du gehst los und ruhst dich die nächsten Tage aus, und ich nehme Daisy mit zu den Partys und Mittagessen, zu denen du gehen würdest."

Kay Bartok sah erleichtert aus. "Ich danke Ihnen, Miss Hamilton, und ich hoffe, wenn ich das nächste Mal vorbeikomme, kann ich Sie besuchen und wir können eine schöne Zeit zusammen verbringen."

Am nächsten Morgen fand sich Daisy in einer Hotelsuite wieder und Mr. Baker half ihr beim Schminken. Daisy war etwas verwirrt.

"Aber Miss Bartok ist älter als ich! Werden die Leute das nicht bemerken? Und was ist mit ihrem Akzent? Ich klinge nicht wie sie."

Lawrence lachte. "Mach dir keine Sorgen, Daisy. Kay ist bekannt für ihr klassisches Bühnen—und Filmschauspiel, sie hat in London studiert, sie klingt englisch und die meisten Leute denken sowieso, dass sie Englisch ist. Dass Kay älter ist als du, sieht sie in ihren Filmen nicht so aus!"

Daisy nahm den Mut an der Hand und fand heraus, dass sie den Rest der Woche unheimlich viel Spaß hatte. Sie trug schöne Kleidung, eröffnete ein Fest, hatte unglaubliches Essen in wunderbaren Restaurants rund um das Herz von London und verdiente fünfhundert Pfund. Lawrence war einer der angenehmsten Menschen, mit denen sie je gearbeitet hat.

Es gab nur ein Problem—leider hatte sie vier Pfund zugenommen! Zurück in ihrem Büro las Daisy die Zeitungen durch, die sie in den letzten Tagen nicht gelesen hatte. Eine Boulevardzeitung las: "Kay Bartok eröffnet ein Fest im Herzen Englands, um Geld für eine Wohltätigkeitsorganisation für Multiple Sklerose zu sammeln. Fast das Doppelte der erwarteten Summe wurde dank dem Charme dieser großen Schauspielerin gespendet. Es wurde festgestellt, dass sie sehr gut aussah, und noch jünger, als sie aussah, als sie Lady Macbeth in Lawrence Baker's Film spielte. Sie sagte bescheiden, dass sie hofft, in ihrer nächsten Rolle noch besser zu spielen und dass sie englisches Eis sehr mag!"

English text:

While having a nice three-flavor ice cream, Daisy gazed at the clothes past the display window of Bronzetti's. She could never go inside the shop though; their prices were too high for her.

"I must admit that Italian styles are very nice, but you have to be pretty slim to get into them," Daisy mused. She was by no means fat, but nor was she skinny. She had a completely average build. Standing there, she thought: "My, doesn't that two-piece have a lovely color."

Behind her, she hears: "Kay, I wasn't expecting to find you here this early—oh, excuse me, I don't think you're Kay, but perhaps you are?"

Daisy looked behind her to see whose voice it was that she was hearing. It was a somewhat rough-looking, bearded man who appeared to be around fifty years of age. He had a dark complexion and sounded like he was from one of the southern states. Despite how modest his clothing looked, he was sporting a famous make of Italian designer glasses, ones she knew to be extremely expensive.

"No, indeed."

Being suddenly spoken to on High Street was not something she was used to, and she made to walk off toward her favourite ice cream shop.

"Please excuse me, Miss... er, you see, I'm a film director and..."

"No, thank you, I'm not interested. Goodbye."

"No, you don't understand. I really am. I'm Lawrence Baker," said the man to Daisy, hoping that the mention of his name would explain his strange behavior.

"And I'm a private investigator!" Daisy retorted.

"Oh, that doesn't matter, you'll do just the same," replied Lawrence.

Daisy was fairly good at shaking off people who look like trouble, but Lawrence's persistence was making her more and more curious.

"My name is Lawrence," the man went on. "Look, in case you've never heard of me, I directed an all-Harlem cast of *The Tempest*."

Daisy had seen Shakespeare on film and had loved it. "Well, I liked your film immensely, but I'm not Kay and... oh, you weren't talking about Kay Bartok, the Canadian actress in *Macbeth*, were you? That was also your film, was it not?

"Yes, it was," Lawrence Baker answered with an amicable smile. It would seem Daisy had made him so very happy. "While my films make very little money, it still gives me pleasure to hear an Englishwoman saying she enjoyed at least one of them. But back to business. I mistook you for Kay. And I've had a wonderful idea. How would you like to be her double for the rest of the week?"

Daisy was nonplussed while Mr. Lawrence went on speaking: "While your face is somewhat dissimilar to hers, you still have a nearly identical build and very similar long brown hair. You know, Kay deserves a well-needed rest. She has been getting a bit rundown lately. She is supposed to be very busy for the next few days with lots of engagements regarding the promotion of our new film *Back to the Jungle with a Modem*."

"Well, I really don't act as a profession—at least, I do sometimes when I'm investigating a case, but..." Daisy said.

"Look, why don't we have a cup of coffee over there," Lawrence pointed toward a small café on the nearby street corner. "Kay is going to that shop to meet me because she wanted to do some shopping first. Look, there she is, going into the coffee shop now."

Lawrence was a very voluble person who would seldom take no as an answer, and Daisy started to become very intrigued by the nature of the events; she had never been offered an opportunity quite like this one. And thus, she and Kay Bartok met. When she and the actress were finally introduced, Daisy noticed that the two had different features and that Kay Bartok appeared to be around fifteen years older than she. But physically, they shared lots of similarities. Kay Bartok's accent was a strong Canadian one.

"So you're a private eye, Miss Hamilton. How very interesting. You must find yourself getting into very dangerous situations from time to time."

Daisy liked this lady because she could see genuine interest in what was said around her in her eyes.

"Kay, what do you think? Miss Hamilton could put on heavy eye makeup and wear a face-covering hat and she would look exactly like you."

"Just a minute, Mr. Baker, I work as a private eye and not as a film double..."

"Look, Daisy, we could pay you just as if you were investigating something. You would be doing us a great favor," Lawrence insisted.

Daisy hesitated; she needed to pay off some office furniture for quite some time and this looked like the quickest route to doing so. Her fax machine had stopped working and there were mountains of files everywhere.

"Well"—she replied—"I was just going on holiday, but I could put it off for a few days."

Lawrence Baker smiled triumphantly: "Kay, you go off and have a rest for the next few days, and I'll take Daisy round with me to the parties and lunches you would be going to."

Kay Bartok appeared to be relieved. "I want to thank you, Miss Hamilton, and I hope the next time I come over, I can look you up and we can have a good time together."

Early the following day, Daisy and Mr. Baker were in a hotel room starting Daisy's makeup. She was a little confused.

"But Miss Bartok is older than I am! Won't people notice? And what about her accent? I sound nothing like her."

Lawrence laughed. "Don't worry, Daisy. Kay is well-known for her stage and film classical acting. She studied in London, you know? She sounds English, and most people think she is English anyway. As to the fact that Kay is older than you, she doesn't look very much older than you in her films!"

Daisy acted very courageously for the remainder of the week and found that she was enjoying herself immensely. She got to wear beautiful clothes, opened a fête, and had great food in lots of great restaurants all around London's center, and all while earning five hundred pounds. Lawrence indeed had been one of the most pleasant people she had ever worked with.

The one problem that she faced was that she now weighed four pounds heavier than before. Upon returning to her office, Daisy began perusing the newspapers she hadn't paid attention to these last few days. She came across a tabloid article which read: "Kay Bartok opens fête in the heart of England to collect money for a multiple sclerosis charity. Nearly double the sum expected was donated thanks to the charm of this great actress. It was noticed that she looked very well, and even younger than she had looked when she played Lady Macbeth in Lawrence Baker's film. She modestly said that she hopes to act even better in her next role and that she likes English ice cream very much!"

Notes:

It's always nice to read a story about someone else's experience that is so far divorced from most people's realities, it almost makes one's head spin. In this fun and very readable anecdote, we caught a glimpse at what is perhaps the more casual side of show-business, the vicissitudes of a director's day-to-day routine.

The text is brief, but it also runs very busily along. The reader is put on even ground with Daisy in that the reader has continual pressure put on them throughout the narrative. The author does a great job of maintaining narrative drive throughout the piece, although it panders off somewhat near the end. But the plot aside, let's now take a look at the grammatical side of things.

Let's start by comparing the first paragraphs of both of these translations. One of the first things that we can take note of is the fact that we are in the past tense and will continue to be for the remainder of the text. German verbs in this tense can usually be conjugated easily.

Let's take a look at some personal pronouns in English along with their German translations to get a better idea of how to decipher all these wild new verbs that are being thrown at us:

English	**German**
I	Ich/I
You	Du
He	Er/e
She	Si
It	Es/s
We	Mir
You (plural)	Ir/r
They (formal)	Si

The very first verb in the story is *looking*: "Daisy was *looking*..." This is a past continuous form of *look*. To get a better idea of German verb conjugation, we will now conjugate the past continuous tense of the verb "look" in English and in German:

English
I-was looking
You-were looking
He-was looking
She-was looking
It-was looking
We-were looking
You(pl)-were looking
They(fr)-were looking

German
Ich/I-Ich schaute
Du-Du hast gesucht
Er/e-Er hat geschaut
Si-Sie schaut
Es/s-Es sah aus
Mir-Mir haben gesucht
Ir/r-Ihr alle guckt euch an
Si-Sie haben gesucht

These are how they're conjugated in the present tense:

English
I-look
You-look
He-looks
She-looks
It-looks
We-look
You(pl)-look
They(fr)-look

German
Ich/I-ich schaue
Du-Sie sehen
Er/e-er sieht aus
Si-Sie sieht aus
Es/s-es sieht aus
Mir-wir schauen
Ir/r-Sie sehen alle aus
Si-Sie gucken

These resources combined should be a valuable asset to us moving forward.

Chapter Two: Die Andernacher Bäckersjungen (The Andernacher Baker Boy)

German text:

Die Andernacher, die Bewohner von Andernach, schlafen bis spät in den Tag hinein, und am Morgen sind die Bäcker die einzigen, die früh aufstehen, damit das frische Brot zum Frühstück fertig ist. Es gab einmal einen Krieg zwischen Andernach und Linz, so dass diese Städte auch heute noch nicht glücklich miteinander sind.

Da die Linzer sehr gut wussten, dass die Andernacher lange schliefen, beschlossen sie, die Stadt früh am Morgen anzugreifen. Alle ihre Pläne waren sehr gut gemacht, und sie glaubten, sie würden gewinnen. Um Mitternacht verließen sie Linz und fuhren ruhig nach Andernach, wo sie sich früh auf den Weg machten, und zwar durch den unkontrollierten Turm der Stadt. In der Zwischenzeit backte die Morgen Bäckerei ihr Brot, und als ihre Arbeit beendet war, setzten sich die Bäcker hin, um ein Nickerchen zu machen.

Als Linzer sich der Stadt näherte, schliefen alle Bewohner, bis auf zwei Bäcker. Sie waren nicht allein. Sie gingen leise aus ihren Häusern, weil sie die Thorax Beuten auf dem Turm entdeckten und den herrlichen Honig probieren wollten. Ohne Lärm zu machen, stiegen sie die Treppe des Turms hinauf, und als sie ankamen, hielten sie an und nahmen ein schönes Stück Honig. Sofort hörten die Jungs ein kleines Geräusch.

"Ah!" flüsterte einer zum anderen. "Die Wache kommt! Er wird uns bestrafen."

Der andere hörte dem Lärm zu und sagte nach einem Moment: "Es kann nicht die Wache sein. Er hat geschlafen! Er würde die Treppe hochgehen. Der Lärm kommt nicht von der Treppe! Es scheint da draußen zu sein."

Leise, sehr leise, weil er nicht beim Honig Klauen erwischt werden wollte, ging er mit einem neugierigen Gesichtsausdruck an den Rand des Turms. Da waren die Linzer, alle bewaffnet, und die Kinder sahen, dass sie ihre Leiter aufstellen wollten, um in die Stadt zu gelangen und die schlafenden Bewohner zu hetzen.

Die Bäcker, die die Gefahr für einen Moment hätten begreifen können, hatten ihren Moment verpasst. Was sollen sie tun? Sie konnten nicht schnell genug aufwachen und hatten keine Waffen, um den Feind zu brechen. Sofort dachte ein Bäcker an den Bienenkorb. Er windet sich leise zu seinen Kameraden. Dann hoben sie den Korb vorsichtig an, brachten ihn an den Rand des Turms und warfen ihn sofort auf den am Fuße des Turms versammelten Linzer.

In Fallen zerbrach der Bienenkorb in Stücke und flog wilde Bienen, die den Linzer bis sie laut schrien. Während die aufgeregten Bienen den Stadtturm verteidigten, stürzten die Bäcker die Treppe hinunter, zogen schnell zum Rathaus, läuteten die große Glocke und weckten alle aus ihrem langen Morgenschlaf. Alle gingen nun zum Turm, um die bedrohte Stadt zu verteidigen, aber ihre Hilfe war nicht mehr nötig, da die Bienen so aggressiv waren, dass die Linzer in Eile geflohen waren.

In Dankbarkeit liefen die Andernacher nach Bildern der beiden Bäckerjungen und brachten sie unter den Stadtturm, den sie so gut verteidigt hatten. Sie sind hier noch zu sehen, weil die anderen das Helganthat noch nicht vergessen haben und oft von dem glücklichen Eingreifen der Bäckerjungen sprechen. Die Linzer kamen nie zurück, um die Stadt zu überstürzen, und sie sagen noch heute, dass die Bienen die Stadt am frühen Morgen bewachen, damit der Rest der Stadt schlafen kann.

English text:

The Andernacher, the residents of Andernach, sleep late into the day, and in the morning, the bakers are the only ones who wake up early so that the fresh bread will be ready for breakfast. There was once a war between Andernach and Linz, so these cities are still not happy with one another today.

Because the Linzer knew very well that the Andernacher slept late, they decided to attack the city early in the morning at one point in time. All their plans were very well laid, and they believed they were going to win. At midnight, they left Linz and went quietly to Andernach, where they made their way early and easily to the city's unchecked tower. Meanwhile, the morning bakers baked their bread, and when their work was finished, the bakers sat down to enjoy a morning nap.

When Linzer approached the city, all the inhabitants were asleep, except for two bakers. They weren't alone. They went quietly out of their homes because they discovered the thorax hives on the tower and wanted to try the splendid honey. Without making noise, they climbed the stairs of the tower, and when they arrived, they stopped, taking a nice piece of honey. At once, the boys heard a little noise.

"Ah!" whispered one to the other. "The guard's coming! He's going to punish us."

The other one listened to the noise and said after a moment: "It can't be the guard. He has been asleep! He would get up the stairs. The noise isn't coming from the stairs! It seems to be out there."

Quietly, very quietly, because he didn't want to be caught stealing honey, he went to the edge of the tower, a curious look on his face. There were the Linzer, all armed, and the kids saw that they wanted to set up their ladder to get into the town and rush the sleeping inhabitants.

The bakers, who had a moment to grasp the danger, had missed their moment to do so. What should they do? They couldn't wake up quickly enough and had no weapons to break the enemy. At once, a baker thought about the bee basket. He winded quietly to his comrades. They then lifted the basket carefully, brought it to the edge of the tower, and threw it all onto the Linzer gathered at the foot of the tower.

In their traps, the bee basket broke into pieces and wild bees flew, stinging the Linzer until they cried aloud. While the excited bees defended the city tower, the bakers rushed down the stairs, moved quickly to the rathaus, tolled the big bell, and woke everyone up from their long morning sleep. Everyone now went to the tower to defend the threatened city, but their help was no longer necessary, because the bees had been so aggressive that the Linzer had fled in haste.

In gratitude, the inhabitants of Andernach ran out for pictures of the two baker's boys, and they brought them under the city tower that they had defended so well. They can still be seen here because the others have not forgotten the Helganthat yet and often speak of the happy intervention of the baker's boys. The Linzer never came back to rush the city, and they still say nowadays that the bees are guarding the city early in the morning so that the rest of the town can sleep.

Notes:

This is a rather strange text that takes us back to a time when the term "warfare" had an entirely different meaning than it does today. It is exciting, nonetheless, to think of cities enclosed by enormous towers, an entire town on the same sleeping schedule, and the defensive line of a hive of bees all in one setting; it is a much-welcome and refreshing break from the realities of modern warfare.

This is a great story, and perhaps one of the more entertaining remembrances of the wars fought in our past. Another lens, and maybe a more personal or useful one, to read this story through is that of a *bildungsroman* featuring a couple of baker's boys whose duty it has become to defend their hometown against a foreign militia. This could be interesting, but the plot doesn't delve into any greater detail about the boys—or any of the characters, for that matter.

One thing that differentiates this story from a number of the other stories in this book is its more highly developed and broadly pronounced narrative arc. It starts off small, like a crack in a dam, with the town as a whole sleeping in. Then, it grows into a tale of an army trying to scale the tower defending the town, just as if the dam is starting, little by little, to give way. Finally, the dam breaks and floods the entire area as the bees fend off the invaders. Afterwards, there is finally, presumably, peace.

As far as grammar is concerned, this would be as good of a time as any to go over definite and indefinite article inflections in German. They are very important tools for learning any language and are relevant throughout every text featured in this book. These inflections are differentiated by their gender—masculine (M), feminine (F), neuter (N), plural (P)—below:

Definite Article Inflection (*the*)

Nominative (the): Der (Mas), Die (Fem), Das (Neu), Die (Plu)
Accusative (the): Den (M), Die (F), Das (N), Die (P)
Genitive (the): Des+s (M), Der (F), Des+s (N), Der (P)
Dative (the): Dem (M), Der (F), Dem (N), Den+m (P)

Indefinite Article Inflections (*a, an*)

Nominative (a, an): Ein (Mas), Eine (Fem), Ein (Neu)
Accusative (a, an): Einen (M), Eine (F), Ein (N)
Genitive (a, an): Eines+s (M), Einer (F), Eines+s (N)
Dative (a, an): Einem (M), Einer (F), Einem (N)

While personal pronouns were touched on in the notes section of the previous chapter, they were only in the present tense and were listed with no mention of gender. We would be remiss not to explore some of the various forms of these pronouns, which may even exceed the aforementioned article inflections (listed above) in importance.

Below are singular and plural personal pronouns, translated from German to English in this case, in their nominative, accusative, genitive, and dative variations.

Singular Tense

Nominative: Ich (I), Du (you), Er (he), Sie (she), Es (it)
Accusative: Mich (me), Dich (you), Ihn (him), Sie (her), Es (it)
Genitive: Mein, Meine (my, mine); Dein, Deine (your, yours); Sein, Seine (his); Ihr, Ihre (her, hers); Sein, Seine (its)
Dative: Mir (me), Dir (you), Ihm (him), Ihr (her), Ihm (it)

Plural Tense

Nominative: Wir (we), Ihr (you), Sie (they), Sie (you)
Accusative: Uns (us), Euch (you), Sie (them), Sie (you)
Genitive: Unser, Unsere (our, ours); Eure, Euer (your, yours); Ihr, Ihre (their, theirs); Ihr, Ihre (your, yours)
Dative: Uns (us), Euch (you), Ihnen (them), Ihnen (you)

Chapter Three: Einkaufen im Supermarkt (Shopping in the Supermarket)

German text:

Frau Meier geht eines Tages in den Supermarkt. Ihr Mann ist nicht zu Hause und sie nimmt den Bus. An der Bushaltestelle trifft sie ihre Freundin Frau Schmidt. Frau Schmidt will auch in den Supermarkt.

Frau Meier: "Das ist toll! Dann können wir zusammen fahren!"

Frau Schmidt: "Ja, das können wir. Und danach können wir Kaffee trinken und Kuchen essen. Im Café neben dem Supermarkt gibt es einen sehr guten Kuchen."

Frau Meier: "Gute Idee!"

Frau Meier und Frau Schmidt gehen zusammen in den Supermarkt.

Frau Meier: "Ich brauche Tomaten. Mein Mann will einen Salat. Ich nehme zehn Tomaten."

Frau Schmidt: "Tomaten sind gut. Ich kaufe fünf Tomaten. Es gibt auch Salat."

Frau Meier nimmt keinen Salat. Aber sie nimmt zwei Gurken. Frau Meier kauft auch ein Kilo Zwiebeln. Frau Schmidt will Brot kaufen.

Frau Meier: "Das Brot hier ist nicht sehr schön, obwohl ich es immer noch in der Bäckerei kaufe. Aber die Schokolade hier ist gut. Es kostet nur 50 Cent. Ich glaube, ich nehme drei Tafeln Schokolade."

Frau Schmidt: "Es gibt ein weiteres Sonderangebot. Mineralwasser und Orangensaft sind billig."

Frau Meier: "Ich habe Orangensaft zu Hause. Aber ich brauche fünf Flaschen Mineralwasser."

Frau Schmidt kauft nur drei Flaschen Mineralwasser. Frau Meier und Frau Schmidt gehen dann zur Kasse. Danach gehen sie ins Cafe. Frau Schmidt trinkt eine Tasse Tee, Frau Meier bevorzugt Kaffee. Sie bestellen zwei Stücke Schokoladenkuchen und nehmen dann den Bus nach Hause.

English text:

Mrs. Meier goes to the supermarket one day. Her husband is not home, and she takes the bus. At the bus stop, she meets her friend Mrs. Schmidt. Mrs. Schmidt also wants to go to the supermarket.

Mrs. Meier: "That's great! Then we can drive together!"

Mrs. Schmidt: "Yes, we can. And afterwards, we can drink coffee and eat cake. In the café next to the supermarket, there is a very good cake."

Mrs. Meier: "Good idea!"

Mrs. Meier and Mrs. Schmidt go to the supermarket together.

Mrs. Meier: "I need tomatoes. My husband wants to have a salad. I'll take ten tomatoes."

Mrs. Schmidt: "Tomatoes are good. I'll buy five tomatoes. There's lettuce, too."

Mrs. Meier does not take lettuce. But she does take two cucumbers. Mrs. Meier also buys a kilo of onions. Mrs. Schmidt wants to buy bread.

Mrs. Meier: "The bread here is not very nice, though I still buy it in the bakery. But the chocolate here is good. It costs only 50 cents. I think I will take three bars of chocolate."

Mrs. Schmidt: "There is another special offer. Mineral water and orange juice are cheap."

Mrs. Meier: "I have orange juice at home. But I do need five bottles of mineral water."

Mrs. Schmidt buys only three bottles of mineral water. Mrs. Meier and Mrs. Schmidt then go to the cash register. Afterwards, they go to the cafe. Mrs. Schmidt drinks a cup of tea, while Mrs. Meier preferred the coffee. They order two pieces of chocolate cake, and then they take the bus home.

Notes:

This brief selection is more valuable in its utility than in its ability to entertain. One would be hard-pressed to find such a short writing so chock-full of useful words and phrases to an ear new to German. It's like vegetables for one's body, or Bach for one's brain.

The most important and most easily notable thing that this text has to offer someone new to German is its food terminology. The foods mentioned are listed below with their German translations in parenthesis:

- Coffee (Kaffee)
- Cake (Kuchen)
- Tomatoes (Tomaten)
- Salad (Salat)
- Lettuce (Grüner Salat)
- Cucumbers (Gurken)
- Onions (Zwiebeln)
- Bread (Brot)

- Chocolate (Schokolade)
- Mineral water (Mineralwasser)
- Orange juice (Orangensaft)
- Tea (Tee)

The other very important terms the text includes are as follows:

- Supermarket (Supermarkt)
- Bus (Bus)
- Bus stop (Bushaltestelle)
- Café (Cafe)
- Bakery (Bäckerei)
- Cash register (Kasse)

Chapter Four: Unser Haus (Our House)

German text:

Ich bin Klara und ich werde Ihnen heute von unserem Haus erzählen. Unser Haus ist sehr groß und hat eine Fläche von 250 Quadratmetern. Wir haben auch einen Garten. Im Garten haben wir viele Blumen und einige Bäume. Im Garten gibt es immer viel zu tun. Ich helfe meinen Eltern gerne dabei, den Überblick zu behalten.

Manchmal kommen Freunde und Familie zu uns nach Hause. Wenn sie es tun, grillen wir im Garten. Es ist immer eine lustige Zeit. Im Haus gibt es zwei Badezimmer. Eines der Badezimmer ist für meine Eltern. Das andere Badezimmer ist für meine Schwester und mich.

Unser Wohnzimmer ist sehr groß und sehr schön. Es gibt ein bequemes Sofa. Neben dem Sofa haben wir einen Tisch und eine Lampe. In der Ecke sitzt ein großer Tisch mit Stühlen, wo wir normalerweise essen. In der Mitte des Raumes befindet sich ein großer Teppich. Der Teppich kommt aus dem Iran. Es gibt auch einen Kamin im Wohnzimmer. Das ist eine sehr gemütliche Sache im Winter und schön warm.

Neben dem Wohnzimmer befindet sich die Küche. Ich mag unsere Küche nicht. Die Möbel sind alt und sehr dunkel. In der Küche gibt es auch einen Esstisch. Unsere Familie isst aber lieber im Wohnzimmer. In der Küche gibt es einen Geschirrspüler, einen Herd und viele Schränke. Es gibt keine Waschmaschine. Die Waschmaschine ist im Keller.

Im ersten Stock befinden sich zwei Kinderzimmer und das Hauptschlafzimmer. Ich finde mein Zimmer schön. Es ist sehr groß und hat weiße Möbel.

English text:

I am Klara, and I'm going to tell you about our house today. Our house is very big, boasting an area of 250 square meters. We also have a garden. In the garden, we have many flowers and some trees. There is always lots of hard work to do in the garden. I like to help my parents in keeping on top of it all.

Sometimes, friends and family come to our house. When they do, we cook barbecue in the garden. It's always a fun time. In the house, there are two bathrooms. One of the bathrooms is for my parents. The other bathroom is for my sister and me.

Our living room is very big and very nice. There is a comfortable sofa. Next to the sofa, we have a table and a lamp. In the corner, there sits a large table with chairs where we usually eat. In the middle of the room is a large carpet. The carpet comes from Iran. There is also a fireplace in the living room. This is a very cozy thing to have in winter, nice and warm.

Next to the living room is the kitchen. I do not like our kitchen. The furniture is old and very dark. In the kitchen, there is also a dining table. Our family prefers to eat in the living room, though. In the kitchen, there is a dishwasher, along with a stove and many cupboards. There is no washing machine. The washing machine is in the basement.

On the first floor are two children's bedrooms and the main bedroom. I think my room is nice. It is very big and has white furniture.

Notes:

This is another example of writing that's more redeeming in its practical application than in its entertainment value. The most important takeaway of this short writing is its household terminology. The places in the house that it mentions are listed below with their German translations in parenthesis:

- Garden (Garten)
- Bathroom (Bad)
- Living room (Wohnzimmer)
- Kitchen (Küche)
- Basement (Keller)
- Children's bedroom (Kinderzimmer)
- Main bedroom (Hauptschlafzimmer)

The other very important terms the text includes are as follows:

- House (Haus)
- Flowers (Blumen)
- Trees (Bäume)
- Table (Tabelle)
- Lamp (Lampe)
- Chairs (Stühle)
- Carpet (Teppich)
- Fireplace (Karmin)
- Dishwasher (Geschirrspüler)
- Stove (Herd)
- Cupboards (Schränke)
- Washing machine (Waschmaschine)
- Furniture (Möbel)

Chapter Five: Die Suche nach Lorna (The Search for Lorna)

German text:

Daisy Hamilton war Privatdetektivin. Sie war dreißig Jahre alt und seit zwei Jahren Detektivin. Jeden Morgen ging sie in ihr Büro, um auf Anrufe zu warten oder die Tür für Kunden zu öffnen, die ihre Dienste benötigen. Daisy war noch nicht sehr bekannt, aber gelegentlich riefen die Leute sie an, nachdem sie die Anzeige in der Lokalzeitung gesehen hatte.

Eines Morgens gegen elf Uhr hört sie jemanden an ihre Bürotür klopfen. Es war eine fette Dame, die ein teures Fell um den Hals trug.

"Hallo, kann ich Ihnen helfen?" fragte Daisy die Dame. "Bitte kommen Sie und setzen Sie sich."

"Oh ja, in der Tat! Ich brauche dringend Ihre Hilfe, Ms. Hamilton. Lorna, meine Kleine ist verschwunden. Ich weiß nicht, was ich tun soll."

Daisy bot der fetten Dame sofort eine Tasse Instantkaffee an und wartete auf die Details. Die fette Dame setzte sich schwer hin und legte ihre große rote Lederhandtasche auf Daisys Schreibtisch.

"Bitte sagen Sie mir alles—Mrs...?"

"Mrs. Edwina Humphries ist mein Name. Ich fürchte, sie werden mich um Geld bitten—ich fürchte, Lorna wurde entführt!"

"Das ist schrecklich, Mrs. Humphries. Denkt Mr. Humphries auch, dass Lorna entführt wurde?"

"Mein Mann ist nicht interessiert, ob Lorna entführt wurde oder nicht!"

"Wirklich, Mrs. Humphries? Aber ist Ihr Mann Lorna's richtiger Vater?"

"Ich weiß nicht, was Sie meinen. Wir haben Lorna zusammen gekauft," antwortete Frau Humphries.

"Sie haben... Mrs. Humphries gekauft, das ist illegal."

"Nein, ist es nicht, nicht in Indien!"

"Du hast Lorna in Indien gekauft?"

"Ja, in der Tat! Und sie hat mir seitdem immer gute Gesellschaft geleistet." Frau Humphries öffnete ihre riesige Ledertasche, um ein Taschentuch herauszuziehen. Mit Entsetzen sah Daisy eine zappelnde Kreatur aus dieser Tasche kommen.

"Mrs. Humphries—bringen Sie das sofort weg!" schrie Daisy.

"Was? Oh Lorna—ich habe dich endlich gefunden," sagte Frau Humphries. "Du hast dich in meiner Tasche versteckt, du böses Mädchen!"

"Mrs. Humphries. Das ist Lorna?"

"Ja, unsere bengalische Sumpfschlange. Oh, danke, meine Liebe. Nein, ich glaube, ich brauche deine Dienste nicht mehr!"

Als Daisy nach Frau Humphries die Tür schloss, machte sie eine geistige Notiz, um in die Anzeige zu schreiben: keine Tiere, keine Schlangen.

English text:

Daisy Hamilton was thirty years old and had been a private detective for the last couple of years. Every morning, she would go to her office to wait for phone calls or to come to the door and receive her clients. Daisy wasn't all that famous yet, but she did have quite a popular ad in the local newspaper; lots of people phoned her because of it.

One morning, at around eleven o'clock, she heard a loud knock at her door. It came from a larger woman, and around her neck, she wore an expensive fur.

"Hello, can I help you?" Daisy asked the lady. "Please come and sit down."

"Oh, yes, indeed! I need your help desperately, Ms. Hamilton. Lorna, my little one has disappeared. I don't know what to do."

Daisy immediately offered a cup of coffee to the fat lady as the two women awaited the details. The lady deposited her large red leather handbag on Daisy's desk and sat heavily down.

"Share everything with me, please—Mrs...?"

"Mrs. Edwina Humphries is my name. I am afraid they will ask me for money—I'm afraid Lorna has been kidnapped!"

"That's terrible, Mrs. Humphries. Does Mr. Humphries, too, think Lorna has been kidnapped?"

"My husband is not interested if Lorna has been kidnapped or not!"

"Really, Mrs. Humphries? But is your husband Lorna's real father?"

"I don't know what you mean. We bought Lorna together," Mrs. Humphries replied.

"You bought... Mrs. Humphries, that's illegal, you know."

"No, it isn't, not in India!"

"You bought Lorna in India?"

"Yes, indeed! And, you know, she has been the best company to me ever since." Mrs. Humphries pulled a handkerchief out of her huge leather bag. Daisy looked on with horror as a wriggling creature came out of the bag.

"Mrs. Humphries—move that away immediately!" Daisy shouted.

"What? Oh, Lorna—I've found you at last!" said Mrs. Humphries. "You hid in my bag—you naughty girl!"

"Mrs. Humphries. This is Lorna?"

"Yes, our Bengali swamp snake. Oh, I do thank you, but it would seem I'll no longer require your services, my dear."

Daisy ushered Mrs. Humphries out and shut the door after her, and as she did she also noted to herself that she should add in her advertisement: no animals, no snakes.

Notes:

Naomi Alderman once said, "Beneath every story, there is another story. There is a hand within the hand... there is a blow behind the blow." This humorous anecdote illustrates that point of meta-storied multiplicity all too effortlessly.

One fascinating quality this story has to offer is its tangible ability to turn an otherwise dull subject matter into a far more memorable experience using irony. Irony, in this case, can be defined as a state of affairs or an event that is often amusing as a result of its being contrary to what one expects. The text begins in a contingent, almost geometric way, and with solidarity. It continues on its path until it explodes into something new: something different with new potentialities. It's always nice to read a plot with this kind of vigor, not necessarily offering satisfaction but always offering meaning.

As mentioned before, unlike its English counterpart, the German language inflects nouns, pronouns, articles, and adjectives into four grammatical cases—Nominative, Accusative, Genitive, and Dative. While German is widely known and considered as a language with more resemblance than dissimilarity to its cousin, the English tongue, the native English speaker new to his or her German textbook often has more difficulty with this disimilarity than he or she does with other aspects of the language. That is why it is very important to be persistent in one's independent study of these cases and their peculiarities.

A few tips in dealing with these sometimes disorienting and befuddling rules and structures are as follows:

The Genitive Case

One rarely uses the genitive case when speaking the language. In fact, the dative case is often substituted for the genitive in conversation. But with this being said, the genitive case will remain more or less obligatory in public speeches, written communication, and any other situation that would not freely give rein to informal language. It is still an unassailablly distinct and definitive part of Germany's *Bildungssprache* (language of education).

In southern German dialects, the use of dative substitutions is more common. The same cannot be said of the German dialects in the northern regions (where Luther's Bible-German had to be learned the way one learns a foreign language) as they more habitually prefer to use the genitive. Though it has been becoming more and more common to neglect the use of the genitive case except when it is formally required to be used, many Germans are aware of how to use it and typically do so. In fact, among the more educated classes, it is even considered a minor embarrassment to be caught using this dative case in an incorrect manner. Thus, for those reasons, it is typically not recommended to avoid learning the genitive case while learning German. It has been gradually falling out of public favor for about 600 years, but it is still far from being extinct.

The Dative Case

For the indirect object of a verb, the dative case is typically used. The dative case also focuses on the location of the object. German speakers place a strong emphasis on the differences between locations and motions; the accusative case is used for the motion of the object and the dative case is for its location.

Chapter Six: Der Hausvater (The Householder)

German text:

Es war einmal ein Mann, der auf Reisen war. Endlich kam er zu einem schönen Haus, das so groß wie ein Palast war.

"Ich konnte gut schlafen," sagte der Mann und ging in den Hofe. Da war ein alter Mann. Der Mann arbeitete daran, Brennholz zu schneiden. "Guten Abend, Vater!" sagte der Reisende. "Guten Abend. Kann ich hier in deinem Haus bleiben?"

"Ich bin nicht der Vater," antwortete der alte Mann in der Hofe, das Holz geteilt. "Betreten Sie das Haus, betreten Sie die Küche. Dort finden Sie meinen Vater. Er wird dir sagen, ob du hier bleiben kannst."

Der Reisende betrat das Haus. Er betrat die Küche und sah einen Mann.

Dieser Mann war alt, er war älter als der Mann, der in der Hofe stand und Holz spaltete. Der alte Mann hat Feuer gemacht.

"Guten Abend, Vater!" sagte der Reisende. "Kann ich hier in deinem Haus bleiben?"

"Ich bin nicht der Vater!" der alte Mann antwortete. "Betreten Sie den Speisesaal. Dort finden Sie meinen Vater. Er sitzt am Tisch und isst."

Der Reisende betrat das Esszimmer. Er sah einen alten, diesmal sehr alten Mann. Er war viel älter als der Mann, der das Feuer in der Küche machte. Der alte Mann saß am Tisch und aß.

"Guten Abend, Vater!" sagte der Reisende. "Kann ich hier bleiben?"

"Ich bin kein Vater! Der alte Mann, der am Tisch saß, hat gegessen. Da ist mein Vater. Er sitzt auf der Bank. Er wird dir sagen, ob du hier bleiben kannst."

Der Reisende ging zur Bank. Da war ein kleiner alter Mann. Er hatte eine lange Pfeife und rauchte.

"Guten Abend, Vater!" sagte der Reisende zu dem kleinen alten Mann, der am Ufer saß und die Pfeife rauchte. "Kann ich hier in deinem Haus bleiben?"

"Ich bin nicht der Vater des Vaters, der kleine alte Mann, der am Ufer saß und die Pfeife rauchte. Da ist mein Vater. Er ist da, im Schlafzimmer. Er liegt im Bett. Er wird dir sagen, ob du hier bleiben kannst."

Der Reisende betrat das Schlafzimmer. Er ist ins Bett gegangen. Da war ein alter, sehr alter Mann, mit zwei großen Augen, die weit offen waren.

"Guten Abend, Vater!" Der Reisende sagte zu dem Mann, der tiefe, offene Augen hatte. "Kann ich hier in deinem Haus bleiben?"

"Ich bin nicht der Vater eines Vaters," sagte der alte Mann, der tief in seinen Augen offen war. "Aber da ist mein Vater. In der Wiege (das Bett eines sehr kleinen Kindes). Er wird dir sagen, ob du hier bleiben kannst."

Der Reisende ist zur Wiege gegangen. Da war ein alter Mann (sehr alt). Er war kaum so groß wie ein sehr kleines Kind und konnte kaum atmen.

"Guten Abend, Vater," sagte der Reisende dem kleinen, alten Mann, der in der Wiege lag und kaum atmen konnte. "Kann ich hier bleiben?"

Ruhig, sehr ruhig, sehr ruhig: "Ich bin nicht der Vater! Mein Vater hängt da an der Wand, im Trinkhorn. Er wird dir sagen, ob du hier bleiben kannst," sagte der alte Mann, der kaum atmen konnte.

Dann ging der Reisende zur Wand. Er sah das Trinkhorn, und es war ein sehr kleiner, alter Mann. Und der Reisende sagte: "Guten Abend, Vater! Kann ich hier in deinem Haus bleiben?"

Dann hörte er den Mann ganz leise sagen: "Ja, mein Kind."

Der Reisende war glücklich. Er saß auf dem Tisch, und es gab gute Dinge zu essen. Er ging ins Bett und konnte gut schlafen. Er saß vor dem Feuer, und er konnte sich gut aufwärmen; und alles war gut, weil er den Vater des alten Vaters fand.

English text:

There was once a man who was traveling. At last, he came to a beautiful house that was as big as a palace.

"I could sleep well," said the man and went to the courtyard. There was an old man. The man was cutting firewood. "Good evening, Father!" said the traveler. "Good evening. Can I stay here in your house?"

"I'm not the father!" the old man answered in the hofe, the wood divided. "Enter the house, enter the kitchen. That's where you find my father. He will tell you if you can stay here."

The traveler entered the house. He entered the kitchen, and he saw a man. This man was old, he was older than the man who stood in the hofe and split wood. The old man made fire.

"Good evening, Father!" said the traveler. "Can I stay here in your house?"

"I'm not the father!" the old man replied. "Enter the dining room.

That's where you find my father. He's sitting at the table and eating."

The traveler entered the dining room. He saw an old, this time very old, man. He was much older than the man who made the fire in the kitchen. The old man sat at the table and ate.

"Good evening, Father!" said the traveler. "Can I stay here?"

"I'm not the father!" The old man who sat at the table was eating. "There's my father. He's sitting on the bank. He will tell you if you can stay here."

The traveler went to the bank. There was a little old man. He had a long whistle and he smoked.

"Good evening, Father!" said the traveler to the little old man who sat on the bank and smoked the pipe. "Can I stay here in your house?"

"I'm not the father's father," said the little old man who sat on the bank and smoked the pipe. "There's my father. He's there, in the bedroom. He's lying in the bed. He will tell you if you can stay here."

The traveler entered the bedroom. He went to bed. There was an old, very old man, with two big eyes that were wide open.

"Good evening, Father!" the traveler said to the man who had open eyes. "Can I stay here in your house?"

"I'm not a father's father," said the old man whose eyes were deeply open. "But there's my father. In the cradle (the bed of a very small child). He will tell you if you can stay here."

The traveler went to the cradle. There was an ancient man (very old). He was hardly as big as a very young child, and he could barely breathe.

"Good evening, Father!" the traveler told the small, ancient man who was in the cradle and could barely breathe. "Can I stay here?"

Quiet, very quiet, very quiet: "I'm not the father! My father hangs there on the wall, in the drinking horn. He will tell you if you can stay here," said the ancient man who could barely breathe.

Then the traveler went to the wall. He saw the drinking horn, and in it was a very small, ancient man. And the traveler said: "Good evening, Father! Can I stay here in your house?"

Then he heard the man very quietly say: "Yeah, my child."

The traveler was happy. He sat on the table, and there were good things to eat. He went to bed and he could sleep well. He sat in front of the fire, and he could warm himself well; and everything was good because he found the old father's father.

Notes:

In its narrative structure, this story is very similar to the one featured in Chapter 5, "Die Suche nach Lorna." The main variance between the two is in their conclusions. Where "Die Suche nach Lorna" ends on an unexpected, comical note, this one ends on a very-much-anticipated and assuring note.

One theme that can be considered throughout this text harkens back to Robert Frost's *After Apple-picking*, about seeing life as a series of opportunities. The traveler wanders through the story looking for the father's father, meeting multiple new people along the way. He meets each and every one of the characters in a different location, all with their own unique features and happenings. He expands through his new experiences and perspectives, and after that, he cannot contract back to the parameters previously put around him.

All throughout the main character's quest for the father of the house, he keeps reciting the interrogative: "Can I stay here?"

Interrogative sentences like these are a highly useful and necessary aspect of any language. Learning how to construct these sentences is an absolute necessity when learning any tongue, especially for the beginner or the casual traveler. The construction of these sentences is not the same in German as it is in English. The pattern for constructing these sentences are listed below:

Supplementary Questions

1. Question word
2. Verb (inflected according to the subject)
3. Subject
4. Other sentence elements

Yes/No Questions

1. Verb (inflected according to the subject)
2. Subject
3. Other sentence elements

Below, we have the common question words in English listed along with their German translations.

English	**Geman**
Who?	Wer?
Who(m)?	Wen?
Who(m)...to?	Wem?
Whose?	Wessen?
What?	Was?
Where?	Wo?
Where...to?	Wohin?
When?	Wann?
How long since?	Seit wann?

From when until when?	Von wann bis wann?
How? What?	Wie?
How much? How many?	Wie viel(e)?
Which? Whichever?	Welche(r/s)?
What a...?	Was fur(ein/e)?
Why?	Warum?

Chapter Seven: Das Reiterbild in Düsseldorf
(The Equestrian Picture in Dusseldorf)

German text:

Ein Künstler lebte einst in Düsseldorf am Rhein. Er war sehr geschickt, so klug, dass der Kurfürst seinen Atem ins Erz goss. Der Künstler war sehr glücklich und arbeitete Tag und Nacht. Endlich war ein Bild fertig und Meister Grupello, der Künstler, brachte es auf den Markt. Als es fertig war, kam der Kurfürst Johann Wilhelm mit all seinen Höfingen. Der Künstler ließ den Schleier fallen, damit jeder das Bild sehen konnte.

Der Kurde, erstaunt über die Schönheit dieses Bildes, gab dem Künstler die Hand und sagte: "Nun, Herr Grupello, Sie haben das sehr gut gemacht. Dieses Bild ist sehr schön. Es ist wirklich tadellos! Du bist ein großer Künstler, und das Bild gibt dir große Ehre!"

Der Künstler war begeistert von diesem Lob, aber die Höflinge, die stillschweigend (ohne ein Wort zu sagen) waren eifersüchtig. Der Fürst hatte ihnen nie eine so freundliche Hand gegeben und sie nie gelobt, und sie alle dachten an sich selbst: "Wie können wir diesen stolzen Künstler demütigen?"

Da der Prinz sein Bild beeindruckend fand, konnten sie nichts Schlechtes darüber sagen, aber endlich sagte der eine: "Ja, Herr Grupello, das Bild des Prinzen ist wirklich makellos. Das Pferd hingegen ist nicht ganz richtig. Schau, der Kopf ist etwas zu groß, das ist nicht ganz natürlich!"

"Nein," sagte der zweite, "das Pferd war nicht so erfolgreich, wie es hätte sein können. Sehen Sie sich den Hals an, Herr Grupello!"

"Ja, und der rechte Fuß ist nicht richtig," sagte der dritte. Der vierte lobte das Bild, aber er rügte den Schwanz des Pferdes. Der fünfte war auch kritisch gegenüber dem Pferd, und nach all ihren Meinungen sagte der Künstler zu dem Prinzen: "Mein Prinz, Ihre Höflinge sind nicht ganz zufrieden mit meiner Arbeit, sie strömen über mich wegen der Pferde."

"Lassen Sie mich ein paar Tage an dem Bild arbeiten, Herr Grupello," antwortete der Kurfürst freundschaftlich. "Bitte tun Sie, was immer Sie für nötig halten. Der Künstler hinterließ den Schleier über dem Bild, und als am nächsten Morgen der Prinz und seine Höflinge zurückkamen, um das Bild wieder zu sehen."

"Oh," dachten alle selbstbewusst. "Ich habe dem Künstler einen guten Rat gegeben. Das Pferd hatte keinen Erfolg. Er hat es selbst gesehen und jetzt ändert er es. Dank meines Ratschlags wird das Bild jetzt wirklich tadellos sein."

Als die Nacht vorbei war, kamen der Kurspreis und seine Höflinge ein zweites Mal, um das Bild zu sehen. Das hohe Brett war verschwunden, und als der Schleier wieder fiel, freute sich der Kurfürst. Dann rief er die Höflinge nacheinander an und fragte sie danach.

Die erste Person, die seinen Kopf geworfen hat, sagte jetzt: "Ah, Herr Kurfürst, das Bild ist jetzt sehr makellos, und Sie sehen den Kopf des Pferdes, jetzt ist er nicht zu groß, aber ganz natürlich."

Der zweite sagte: "Ja, das Bild ist jetzt sehr makellos. Der Hals des Pferdes ist jetzt sehr gnädig."

Der dritte sagte: "Da Sie den rechten Fuß gewechselt haben, Herr Grupello, ist Ihr Bild einwandfrei."

Alle waren jetzt sehr glücklich, und der Kurde erzählte dem Künstler, der still war, "Herr Grupello, alle diese Herren sind jetzt zufrieden mit Ihrer Arbeit und loben Ihre Veränderungen am Pferd."

"Herr Kurfürst," antwortete der Künstler, "ich bin sehr froh, dass alle mit meinem Bild so zufrieden sind, aber ich muss zugeben, dass ich daran nichts geändert habe. Ein Bild kann nicht verändert werden. Trotzdem habe ich euch jetzt alle gehört."

Der Kurfürst war überrascht. "Über was hast du geredet?"

"Über den Ruf Ihrer Höflinge, Herr Fürst, der auf der Suche nach dem Bild der Eifersucht war, und ich glaube, das ist jetzt völlig zerstört!"

Die Höflinge konnten sich nicht revanchieren, und sie alle setzten ihre Kritik fort. Das Bild ist immer noch das Herzstück des Düsseldorfer Marktes, wo es jeder bewundern kann.

English text:

An artist once lived in Dusseldorf on the Rhine. He was very skillful, so clever that the Kurfürst "poured his breath into the ore." The artist was very happy and worked day and night. At last, a picture was finished and Master Grupello, the artist, put it on the market. When it was complete, the Kurprince Johann Wilhelm came to see it with all his courtiers. The artist dropped the veil so everyone could see the picture.

The prince, astonished by the beauty of this image, gave the artist his hand and said: "Now, Mr. Grupello, you have done this very well. This picture is very beautiful. It really is impeccable! You are a great artist, and the picture gives you great honor!"

The artist was delighted with this praise, but the courtiers who were taciturn (without saying a word) were jealous. The prince had never given them such a friendly hand or praised them, and they all thought to themselves: "How can we humiliate this proud artist?"

Since the prince found his image impressive, they couldn't say anything bad about it, but at last one said: "Yes, Mr. Grupello, the image of the prince is really impeccable. The horse, on the other hand, is not quite right. Look, the head is a little too big, it's not quite natural!"

"No," the second said, "the horse did not succeed as well as it could have. Look at the neck, Mr. Grupello!"

"Yes, and the right foot isn't right," said the third. The fourth praised the picture, but he reprimanded the horse's tail.

The fifth was also critical of the horse and, after all their opinions, the artist said to the prince: "My Prince, your courtiers are not entirely satisfied with my work, they are pouring onto me about the horses. Are you going to let me work on the picture for a few days?"

"If you like, Mr. Grupello," the Kurfürst responded amicably. "Please do to it whatever you deem necessary."

The artist left the veil over the picture, and when the next morning approached, the prince and his courtiers came back to see the picture again.

"Oh," all of them thought to themselves with confidence. "I gave the artist a good advice. The horse didn't succeed at all. He saw it himself, and now he changed it. Thanks to my advice, the picture will now be really impeccable."

When the night was over, the prince and his courtiers came to see the picture a second time. The high plank had disappeared, and when the veil fell again, the prince was rejoicing. Then he called the courtiers, one after the other, and asked them about it. The first person who threw his head said now: "Ah, my prince, the picture is now very impeccable. And look at the head of the horse, now he is not too big, but quite natural."

The second said: "Yes, the picture's very impeccable now. The neck of the horse is now very graceful."

The third said: "Since you have changed the right foot, Mr. Grupello, your picture is perfect."

Everyone was very happy now, and the Kurprince told the artist who was silent, "Mr. Grupello, all these gentlemen are now satisfied with your work; they all praise your changes to the horse."

"My prince," the artist replied, "I am quite happy that everyone is so pleased with my picture, but I have to admit that I have not changed anything about it. A picture cannot be changed. Nevertheless, I have heard you all now."

The prince was surprised. "What are you talking about?"

"The reputation of your courtiers, my prince, who was looking for the image of jealousy. And I think that is now completely destroyed!"

The courtiers couldn't reciprocate, and they all continued with their criticisms. The picture is still at the heart of the market in Dusseldorf, where everyone can admire it.

Notes:

This is a very fascinating story. Anyone who has ever found themselves criticised unjustifiably by others might easily relate, especially if the critics had been remiss to consider the best interest of the one being criticized. Anyone who has ever felt alienated among peers, or perhaps conspired against, will almost invariably take this story to heart. Arguably the most important action of this story is Mr. Grupello's maturity and grace in silencing his pedantic tormentors.

The second half of the story where the prince and his harsh courtiers come back to reexamine the picture begins with the courtiers at last praising the picture. But the love they bestow is ultimately unveiled as an illusion brought on by confirmation bias after Mr. Grupello reveals that he had made no changes to the picture, explaining that "a picture can not be changed."

This really is a great example of what to do when one is being brought down by others who are willing to blow hot or cold at any given thing based on what the others among their peers decide. As soon as the first courtier gave an opinion and took leadership of the rest, the prospect of the painter having a fair trial vanished, and with it went the other courtier's abilities to think for themselves. That is the main reason that this story is a classic, even though it may not be the most well-known story in the world or even in this book. Its content has a relatability in any era.

One very important aspect of the German language is the subject of phrases. This is of particular importance to the native English speaker because German uses a process called declension which English does not. An example of this process is shown below:

Mary reads a book. She reads a book.

"Mary" is the subject of the phrase, and "she" also happens to be in the nominative case. The reader can ask "who?" after the subject of this phrase. Who is it who reads the book? It is Mary.

This phrase's subject defines its verb. Mary happens to be in the third person singular tense right now. If we were to change the phrase into the first person plural, for example, then the verb would change with it as well.

Chapter Eight: Der Pfannkuchen (The Pancake)

German text:

Es war einmal eine Frau, die sieben hungrige Kinder hatte. Sie machte einen Pfannkuchen für die hungrigen Kinder. Es war ein großer Pfannkuchen, aus süßer Milch gemacht, und er lag in der Pfanne auf dem Feuer.

Die Kinder, die so hungrig waren, standen alle da und das erste Kind sagte: "Ach, Mutter, ich bin so hungrig, gieb mir ein Stück Pfannkuchen."

"Ach, gute Mutter!" sagte das zweite Kind. "Ich bin auch hungrig, gieb mir auch ein Stück Pfannkuchen."

"Ach, liebe, gute Mutter!" sagte das dritte Kind. "Ich bin auch hungrig. Gieb mir ein Stück Pfannkuchen."

"Ach, süße, gute, liebe Mutter," sagte das vierte Kind. "Ich habe auch Hunger. Ich möchte auch ein Stück Pfannkuchen haben."

"Liebe, gute, süße, kleine Mutter," rief (sagte laut) das fünfte Kind. "Ich möchte auch ein Stück Pfannkuchen haben."

Und das sechste Kind rief: "Geschickte, gute, süße, liebe, kleine Mutter, laß mich auch ein Stück Pfannkuchen haben. Ich habe auch Hunger."

Und das siebente und letzte Kind rief: "Geschickte, gute, süße, liebe, niedliche, kleine Mutter, laß mich auch ein Stück Pfannkuchen haben. Ich habe auch Hunger."

"Ja, ja, meine Kinder," antwortete die Frau. "Wartet nur, bis der Pfannkuchen auf der anderen Seite gebacken ist. Seht, er ist so schön und wird so gut zu essen sein."

Als der Kuchen das hörte, fürchtete er sich sehr und drehte sich schnell um. Jetzt konnte er auch auf der anderen Seite backen. Nach einigen Minuten war der Pfannkuchen gebacken, aber da er sich so sehr fürchtete, sprang er aus der Pfanne. Er sprang auf den Boden und rollte schnell aus dem Hause.

"Halt, Pfannkuchen, halt!" rief die Mutter.

"Halt, Pfannkuchen, halt!" riefen die sieben Kinder.

Aber der Kuchen rollte schnell weiter. Die Frau und alle sieben Kinder liefen ihm nach, aber er rollte so schnell, daß sie ihn bald nicht mehr sehen konnten. Der Pfannkuchen rollte weiter und weiter, und endlich begegnete er einem alten Manne.

"Guten Tag, Pfannkuchen!" rief der Mann.

"Gott behüte Sie!" antwortete der Pfannkuchen.

"Rollen Sie nicht so schnell, lieber Pfannkuchen. Warten Sie. Ich möchte Sie essen!"

"Ach!" antwortete der Pfannkuchen. "Ich muß schnell fortrollen, denn die Frau mit den sieben hungrigen Kindern kommt, um mich zu essen!"

Und der Pfannkuchen rollte weiter, und der Mann folgte ihm. Endlich begegnete der Pfannkuchen einer Henne.

"Guten Morgen, Pfannkuchen," rief die Henne.

"Gott behüte Sie!" antwortete der Pfannkuchen.

"Ach, lieber Pfannkuchen!" rief die Henne. "Rollen Sie doch nicht so schnell. Warten Sie doch eine Minute, ich möchte Sie fressen."

"Ich kann nicht warten, ich muß weiter rollen," antwortete der Pfannkuchen, "denn die Frau mit den sieben hungrigen Kindern und der Mann wollen mich haben."

Und der Pfannkuchen rollte schnell weiter, und die Henne folgte ihm.

Dann begegnete der rollende Pfannkuchen einem Hahne.

"Guten Tag, lieber Pfannkuchen," rief der Hahn.

"Gott behüte Sie!" antwortete der Pfannkuchen und rollte weiter.

"Lieber Pfannkuchen," sagte der Hahn. "Warten Sie doch eine Minute. Ich möchte Sie fressen."

"Ich kann ja nicht warten," antwortete der Pfannkuchen, "ich muß weiter rollen, denn die Frau mit den sieben hungrigen Kindern, der Mann und die Henne folgen mir alle!"

Der Pfannkuchen rollte weiter, und der Hahn folgte ihm auch.

Dann begegnete der Pfannkuchen einer Ente.

"Guten Tag, Pfannkuchen," rief die Ente.

"Gott behüte Sie!" antwortete der Pfannkuchen.

"Aber, lieber Pfannkuchen, gehen Sie doch nicht so schnell!" rief die Ente. "Warten Sie. Ich möchte Sie fressen."

"Ich kann nicht warten!" antwortete der Pfannkuchen. "Da kommt die Frau mit den sieben hungrigen Kindern, der Mann, die Henne, der Hahn, und alle, alle wollen mich haben."

Der arme Pfannkuchen rollte weiter, und die Ente folgte ihm auch.

Endlich begegnete er einer Gans.

"Guten Tag, Pfannkuchen," rief die Gans.

"Gott behüte Sie!" antwortete der Pfannkuchen.

"Aber, lieber Pfannkuchen, rollen Sie doch nicht so schnell!" rief die Gans. "Warten Sie doch. Ich möchte Sie fressen!"

"Warten, ich kann nicht warten," antwortete der Pfannkuchen. "Da kommt die Frau mit den sieben hungrigen Kindern, der Mann, die Henne, der Hahn und die Ente, und alle wollen mich haben. Hier kann ich nicht bleiben. Ich muß weiter rollen!"

Der Pfannkuchen rollte weiter und die Gans lief ihm nach (folgte ihm).

Dann begegnete er einem Gänserich.

"Guten Tag, lieber Pfannkuchen!" rief der Gänserich.

"Gott behüte Sie!" antwortete der Pfannkuchen.

"Lieber Pfannkuchen, rollen Sie doch nicht so schnell!" rief der Gänserich. "Warten Sie eine Minute. Ich möchte Sie fressen!"

"Ach, ich kann ja nicht!" antwortete der Pfannkuchen. "Da kommt die Frau mit den sieben hungrigen Kindern, der Mann, die Henne, der Hahn, die Ente und die Gans, und alle, alle wollen mich haben. Darum kann ich nicht warten! Darum muß ich schnell weiter rollen!"

Und der Pfannkuchen rollte schnell weiter, und der Gänserich lief ihm nach.

Endlich begegnete der Pfannkuchen einem Schweine.

"Guten Tag, Pfannkuchen," sagte das Schwein.

"Gott behüte Sie!" antwortete der rollende Pfannkuchen.

"Warten Sie doch eine Minute, lieber Pfannkuchen!" rief das Schwein. "Ich möchte Sie fressen, und Sie gehen zu schnell."

"Ach, liebes Schwein, ich kann ja nicht warten. Die Frau mit den sieben hungrigen Kindern, der Mann, die Henne, der Hahn, die Ente, die Gans und der Gänserich kommen alle, um mich zu nehmen. Ich kann nicht warten." Und der Pfannkuchen rollte weiter und das Schwein lief ihm nach.

"Halt!" rief das Schwein. "Hier ist ein Wald, lieber Pfannkuchen. Im Walde sind nichts als Bäume. Da werden Sie sich fürchten!"

"Ja, das ist wahr (so)," antwortete der Pfannkuchen. "Im Walde, wo nichts als Bäume sind, werde ich mich fürchten."

"Gehen wir zusammen (beide) durch den Wald!" sagte das Schwein.

"Ach, ja, das ist ein guter Einfall!" rief der Pfannkuchen, und sie gingen zusammen.

Endlich kamen sie an einen Bach (ein sehr kleiner Strom). Das Schwein war so fett, daß es sehr gut schwimmen konnte. Aber der arme Pfannkuchen konnte nicht schwimmen. Dann sagte er zu dem Schweine: "Ach, mein lieber Freund, ich kann nicht schwimmen. Ich kann nicht über den Bach kommen!"

"Ach!" sagte das Schwein. "Es ist schade, daß Sie nicht schwimmen können. Aber springen Sie doch auf meinen Kopf, so werden Sie gut hinüber kommen."

"Das ist eine gute Idee!" sagte der Pfannkuchen, und er sprang auf den Kopf des Schweines.

Als das Schwein im Bach war, öffnete es den Mund und fraß den armen Pfannkuchen. Und, da der arme Pfannkuchen nicht weiter gehen konnte, so kann diese Geschichte auch nicht weiter gehen und muß hier enden.

English text:

Once upon a time, there was a woman who had seven hungry children. She made a pancake for the hungry kids. It was a big pancake, made of sweet milk, and she laid it in the pan on the fire.

The children who were so hungry were all standing there and the first child said: "Oh, mother, I'm so hungry, give me a piece of that pancake."

"Oh, good mother!" said the second child. "I'm also hungry, give me a piece of the pancake, too."

"Oh, dear, good mother!" said the third child. "I'm hungry, too. Give me a piece of the pancake."

"Oh, sweet, good, dear mother," said the fourth child. "I'm hungry, too. I'll have a piece of the pancake as well."

"Lovely, good, sweet, little mother," shouted (said aloud) the fifth child. "I want a piece of the pancake, too."

And the sixth child shouted: "Skillful, good, sweet, dear, little mother, let me also have a piece of the pancake. I'm hungry, too."

And the seventh and last child shouted: "Skillful, good, sweet, dear, cute, little mother, let me also have a piece of the pancake. I'm hungry, too."

"Yes, yes, my children," the woman replied. "Wait till the pancake's baked on the other side. Look, he is so beautiful and will be so good to eat."

When the cake heard that, he was very afraid and turned around quickly. Now he could also bake on the other side. After a few minutes, the pancake was baked, but because he was so afraid, he leaped right out of the pan. He jumped to the floor and quickly rolled out of the house.

"Stop, pancake, stop!" called the mother.

"Stop, pancake, stop!" the seven children shouted.

But the cake kept rolling fast. The wife and all seven children ran after him, but he rolled so fast that soon they could no longer see him. The pancake rolled on and on, and finally he met an old man.

"Hello, pancake!" the man shouted.

"God bless you!" replied the pancake.

"Don't roll so fast, dear pancake. Hold on, hold on. I want to eat you!"

"Alas!" answered the pancake. "I must hurry, for the woman with the seven hungry children are coming to eat me!"

And the pancake kept rolling, and the man followed him. Finally, the pancake met a hen.

"Good morning, pancake," the hen shouted.

"God bless you!" replied the pancake.

"Oh, dear pancake!" the hen shouted. "Don't roll so fast. Wait a minute, I want to eat you."

"I can't wait, I have to keep rolling," the pancake replied, "because the woman with the seven hungry children and the man want me."

And the pancake rolled on quickly, and the hen followed him.

Then the rolling pancake met a cockerel.

"Good day, dear pancake," the rooster shouted.

"God bless you!" the pancake replied and rolled on.

"Dear pancake," said the rooster. "Just wait a minute. I want to eat you."

"I can't wait," the pancake replied, "I have to keep rolling, because the woman with the seven hungry children, the man, and the hen are all following me!"

The pancake kept rolling, and the rooster followed.

Then the pancake met a duck.

"Hello, pancake," the duck shouted.

"God bless you!" replied the pancake.

"But, dear pancake, don't go so fast!" the duck shouted. "Wait, wait. I want to eat you."

"I can't wait!" replied the pancake. "Here comes the woman with the seven hungry children, the man, the hen, the rooster, and everyone, they all want me."

The poor pancake rolled on, and the duck followed him, too.

He met a goose.

"Hello, pancake," the goose shouted.

"God bless you!" replied the pancake.

"But, dear pancake, don't roll so fast!" the goose shouted. "Wait, please. I want to eat you!"

"Wait, I can't wait," the pancake replied. "Here comes the woman with the seven hungry children, the man, the hen, the rooster, and the duck, and they all want me. I can't stay here. I have to keep rolling!"

The pancake rolled on and the goose followed him.

Then he met a gander.

"Good day, dear pancake!" the gander shouted.

"God bless you!" replied the pancake.

"Dear pancake, don't roll so fast!" shouted the gander. "Wait a minute. I want to eat you!"

"Oh, I can't!" replied the pancake. "Here comes the woman with the seven hungry children, the man, the hen, the rooster, the duck, and the goose, and all of them want me. That's why I can't wait! I have to keep rolling!"

And the pancake rolled on quickly, and the gander ran after him.

Finally, the pancake met a pig

"Hello, pancake," said the pig.

"God bless you!" replied the pancake on wheels.

"Wait a minute, dear pancake!" the pig shouted. "I want to eat you, and you walk too fast."

"Oh, dear pig, I can't wait. The woman with the seven hungry children, the man, the hen, the cock, the duck, the goose, and the gander all come to take me. I can't wait." And the pancake kept rolling and the pig ran after him.

"Stop!" the pig shouted. "Here's a forest, dear pancake. There's nothing but trees in the forest. You'll be scared!"

"Yes, that's true," the pancake replied. "In the forest, where there are only trees, I will be afraid."

"Let's go together (both of us) through the forest!" said the pig.

"Oh, yeah, that's a good idea!" the pancake shouted, and they left together.

Finally, they came to a stream (a very small river). The pig was so fat that it could swim very well. But the poor pancake couldn't swim. Then he said to the pig: "Oh, my dear friend, I can't swim. I can't get across the creek!"

"Ah!" said the pig. "It's a pity you can't swim. Why don't you jump on my head and get across it with me?"

"That's a good idea!" said the pancake, and he jumped on the pig's head.

When the pig was in the creek, it opened its mouth and ate the poor pancake. And, since the poor pancake couldn't go any further, this story can't go any further and must end here.

Notes:

To end the series of stories on a humorous note, I've included the short story entitled "Der Pfannkuchen," which you have just read. Not only is this story remarkable in its Germanic gallows humor, deadpanning its way through a pancake's quest to get away from a family that wants to eat it, but it's also remarkable in the multitude of messages that can be taken from it.

The idea of a pancake, doomed from the onset to a destiny of being eaten, and running away from all its predators is one that is very dynamic. It's something of a Peter Pan story that has been told and retold in many different times and places. But a central theme that stays intact throughout all the different transcriptions is that the problems one faces always have a way of multiplying and eventually swallowing the sufferer whole if he or she simply runs away from them time and time again. Additionally, a pig helping a pancake cross a creek just isn't a great strategy for growth, however hilarious it may be.

One aspect of the German language which hasn't been discussed in depthly yet is the pronunciation of characters and words. While German is a very similar language to English and most of what is written in German can be pronounced naturally by an English speaker, there still remains some variance in pronunciation. Some pronunciation issues and examples the native English speaker often comes across are listed below.

The R sound: The sound of the German "r" is one of the sounds that lead listeners to judge that the language is ugly. It is produced by the medulla oblongata vibrating in the back of one's throat.

German, English: (Rot, Red), (Rose, Rose)

The V and W sounds: The V in German can actually produce two different sounds. One is similar to the F in German (and also in English). In essence, they have two letters which can produce the same sound (F).

German V pronounced as English F: (Vogel, Bird), (Vorsicht, Care)

Then again, the V can also share the same sound as the V in English (or, in German, a W). So the W and F sounds in German have two possibilities for expression, with W=V and F=V.

V pronounced like the English V: (Vase, Vase), (Klavier, Piano)

V pronounced like the English F: (Vetter, Cousin), (Vollmond, Full Moon)

The Umlaute ä, ö, ü: To most of us around the world who cannot claim German as our mother language, these sounds might prove to be the most challenging to pronounce. How one can pronounce a character that is not even found on most keyboards is the question here.

The "ä" is not too much of a struggle. However, when hearing both ä and e sounds spoken, it is not easy to distinguish between them. The short ä sounds like the E letter in the English words gender, men, or let.

The ö sound is quite close to the O sound in English, but with the former, the lips should be kept a little bit closer together. In fact, it makes the same sound one would when pronouncing fur, burden, or murder.

The ü may be the most challenging one to pronounce among those listed here because it has no close equivalent in the English language. Imagine if the English U were to meet a long ee: your lips are positioned as if you were about to whistle, yet instead of whistling, you then started to speak.

Some examples containing these three sounds are listed below:

Ä, ä: (ähnlich, similar), (Ärger, trouble)
Ö, ö: (öffentlich, public), (Öl, oil)
Ü, ü: (über, over), (Lüge, lie)

The SCH sound: These three letters form one sound in German, comparable with the English sh.

(Schöne, Nice), (Schuh, Shoe)

The CH sound: These two letters actually form one compound sound in the form of two different sounds in German; one is more and the other is less guttural. Few English words have a more guttural sound, and one of them is the famous Loch Ness. Remember the sound of ch in Loch as that is exactly what we are looking for.

More guttural ch: (Kachel, Tile), (Bach, Stream)

And then there is the ch sound that is less guttural. The difficulty here lies in the fact that there is nothing in English that this can be compared to. Try this: take the sound sh (as in shiver) and move the corners of your mouth outwards. You should come across a hissing sound, which should be something similar to the sounds of the following examples:

Less guttural ch: (Ich, I), (Gicht, Gout)

The SS/ß sound: Here, we once again come across an example of two different means of writing out one sound. Luckily for us, it's nothing too advanced. It's simply your standard "s" sound, as in sauce or song. But as every language does, the German language has a history, so while this character may be redundant, it is kept for the sake of tradition.

ss/ß: (Er hieß, his name was), (weiß, white)

Follow this orthographic rule for when to use which one of these spellings: After long diphthongs and long vowels, use ß; after short vowels, use ss.

What is a vowel?

Vowels in the German language constitute all the sounds which are not consonants (an explanation that is only marginally helpful, I admit), and they are also the letters that sound in of themselves. There are eight vowels in German: a, e, i, o, u, ä, ö, ü.

As you know, the sounds in between the vowels are consonants. Consonants can only be put together because of vowels, to an extent. Otherwise we would only have words like in the first example listed below. The second example is easy to pronounce, especially when compared to the first. Note that both examples are invented. They don't mean a thing (at least not in German).

Impossible to pronounce: Brgm
Easy to pronounce: Barogem

Short and long vowels

In German, just like in English, there are short vowels and there are long vowels. Some examples are listed below.

Short vowels: (Offen, Open), (Ass, Ace), (Suppe, Soup), (Bett, Bed), (Widder, Aries)

Long vowels: (Ofen, Oven), (Aas, Carrion), (Super, Super), (Beet, Flower bed), (Wieder, Again)

Some differences can be distinguished between these types of vowels. Between the pairs Ofen/Ofenn, Aas/Ass, Beet/Bett, and Widder/Wieder, there is one distinct difference: either the vowel is long or it is short. Their meanings are completely different though, and it is of great importance to know these differences. Short and long vowels are marked in certain ways in written German.

***Ie** for long i*: (Wiese, Meadow), (Liegen, To lie down), (Wiegen, To weigh)
***Aa** for long a*: (Aal, Eal), (Saal, Hall)

A vowel that is followed by an H becomes a long vowel: (Die Ahnen, Ancestors), (Etwas Ahnen, To suspect)
O: (Ohne, Without), (Ohr, Ear)
E: (Ehrliche, Honesty), (Ehre, Honor)

These examples do not contain any indication of whether the vowel is short or long: (Schaf, Sheep), (Laden, Shop), (Frage, Question)

If the vowel has a ß after it, then it will be long: (Straße, Street), (Stoß, Hit/Push), (Muße, Leisure)

A short vowel may be indicated by two consonants following it: (Immer, Always), (Essen, Eat), (Pass, Passport), (Müssen, To must)

Diphthongs (ei, ai, au): (Elmer, Bucket), (Seife, Soap), (Mai, May), (Sauer, Sour), (Bauer, Farmer), (Maus, Mouse)

The Z sound: Z in German makes the same sound as "ts" in English

(Zug, Train), (Ziehen, To pull), (Zeige, Goat)

The TZ sound: This sound is similar to the sound that Z makes. The main variance is a slight pronunciation of T.

Tz, Z: (Sitzen, To sit), (Siezen, To address someone formally), (Sitz, Seat), (Plütze, Puddle), (Platz, Place)

Note, however, that **ZT** is to be pronounced slightly differently: (Arzt, Doctor), (Er sitzt, He is sitting), (Er siezt uns, he formally addresses us)

Conclusion

Thank you for making it through to the end of *German Short Stories and Their English Translations*. I hope you enjoyed it and learned something along the way. Learning the German language (or any language, for that matter) is an endeavor that requires many hours of committed work if you are to reap any great rewards. The subject of German is one with a surface that cannot even be scratched within the narrow confines of these few pages. To properly learn German, the reader would need to continue to study, potentially for years. This book was meant to be a helpful guide for the beginner stages of the journey.

The reader's next step in his or her education would be to search for other resources to become more educated on the subject. The resources to be found are innumerable and are easily accessible. There are also some websites which provide side-by-side translations of texts in nearly all languages the world has to offer, all of which would be valuable assets to the reader moving forward.

Some tips to keep in mind when learning a new language would be to know what your goal is, as it is much easier to stay motivated when you have a clear purpose for what you are doing. You must also be clear on what the topic has to offer to you as the student. Speak with a partner or just with yourself for practice. Doing this can help you discover, refresh, and retain words and phrases in your mind, as well as build confidence in your abilities to reach your goal. Listen to the language as spoken by a native; make certain words and phrases concrete in your mind using repetition and familiarity. Most importantly of all, have fun! You won't want language-learning to become just another chore.

Finally, if you found this book useful in any way, a review on Amazon would be greatly appreciated!

www.ingramcontent.com/pod-product-compliance
Lightning Source LLC
Chambersburg PA
CBHW052131110526
44591CB00012B/1681